Multiflow Computer

To John
with many thanks

[signature]

Multiflow Computer

A Start-up Odyssey

Elizabeth Fisher

http://www.MultiflowTheBook.com

For Josh, now and always

CONTENTS

PREFACE

This is a story I have always wanted told. For years I begged Josh to write it, but he is a scientist and this story is not about science or, really, even about technology. Gene Pettinelli, the Multiflow lead investor, asked Josh to give talks about the company but he always refused. He never understood what we found so fascinating, never understood the appeal. Bob Rau, Josh's colleague at Hewlett-Packard who founded a Multiflow competitor, always said that a start-up was a fabulous thing to have done—once. And that was Josh's attitude: it was an amazing experience but exhausting, and only the technology interested him.

Josh is my husband, Joseph A. Fisher: computer scientist, retired Hewlett-Packard Senior Fellow, former Yale professor, Eckert-Mauchly award winner. He invented a new computer architecture in his PhD thesis at NYU and developed it as a young faculty member at Yale. He thought his radically different approach to computer design would revolutionize the world of scientific computing, and he came nearer to realizing that dream than seems possible.

Josh put his heart into Multiflow, even though the role he took wasn't doing science and he had to venture into management. During these years, I watched him change with blinding speed from a scruffy graduate student with working-class roots to a respected scientist and seasoned senior executive. It was a truly remarkable transformation.

1

Multiflow Computer, Inc. was a computer start-up, founded in 1984 to commercialize Josh's VLIW technology. It was funded by venture capital, founded by Josh and by John O'Donnell and John Ruttenberg, both also from Yale. The company manufactured computers, selling and distributing them nationally and internationally, until it went out of business six years after its founding. It raised about $60 million of venture capital, sold about 140 machines at an average price of around $350,000 and had about 170 employees at its end. One of the computers, a Multiflow Trace, now lives in the Computer Museum in Mountain View, California.

When Josh first publicly proposed VLIW technology in 1983, his scientific colleagues thought it wouldn't work, that you couldn't build a general purpose computer to run any scientific program with speed-up coming from the software not the hardware. This radically different computer design was too strange for many of his colleagues; everyone was skeptical.

Jim Goodman, Chair of Computer Science at the University of Wisconsin, saw the first VLIW presentation in Stockholm. "When I first heard it, I thought it was the most 'blue sky' idea ever, and the next thing I knew, there was a working product." Jim said it was the most amazing thing he had ever seen.

What made Josh and his colleagues think they could completely change the computer industry? They were young, of course, and had the arrogance of youth, but the 1980s was also a time for grandiose ideas in the computer world. Computer science was a new science then and the rules were just being written. The way computers were used was changing quickly; companies with new technologies were popping up every day. It was the Wild

West, fun, with new discoveries everywhere. It seemed that anything could happen.

Josh and his colleagues had no idea what they were getting into when they started Multiflow. They learned as they went along, making their way in the industrial world, unfamiliar as it was to most of them. Multiflow had timing on its side, and a lot of luck, and whether any good idea can survive to change the world depends as much on luck as on the superiority of the idea. Ultimately, though, they never sold enough computers to be profitable and the administration and sales efforts weren't up to the stellar quality of the engineering. Then the changing nature of the computer industry, which helped at first, swept over Multiflow and drove it and its whole industry segment under. It was "the attack of the killer micros," the beginning of the technological convergence that continues today, that made the computers Multiflow produced— powerful mini-supercomputers—unnecessary for most of scientific computing.

The work was hard, a roller coaster of emotional highs and lows—the travel, the craziness, raising money, the selling—but if it had succeeded, Josh never would have left. For him it was very personal and, really, a dream—all those amazingly talented people at Multiflow working on his technology, on his vision. He wanted to change the world of scientific computing and they were making it happen.

The story of Multiflow is also about the remarkable people who worked there, the people who went on to become stars in the computer industry. This was a group of very smart and talented young engineers—first rate computer scientists every one of them—full of drive and strong opinions, believing in the technology and creating the product. They worked hard, working with people who were at the same genius level of intelligence as they were, people who would be stars anywhere—with management completely behind them. It was paradise for these smartest of engineers.

Besides Josh, the company produced another Eckert-Mauchly award winner and three other industrial Fellows. Even many of the non-engineers were outstanding. Mike Loukides, a Stanford English PhD who wrote the documentation, went on to become a Senior Editor at O'Reilly Media, a prominent publisher of technical books, after Multiflow folded. He is now their Vice President of Content Strategy.

I had a peripheral role at the company, first finding office space and employee benefits and then producing the presentation graphics used in fundraising and sales. But mostly my role was to be Josh's wife, listening, amazed at the scale of what was happening. This is how I heard the whole Multiflow story, from Josh at our dinner table and in phone calls from every part of the world when he was on the road. I thought Multiflow was the most exciting thing I had ever been a part of. Josh and I have been telling each other these stories for the past twenty-five years.

People have asked me whether Multiflow made my family rich and the answer is no, or not directly. Josh invented the technology but because it is an architectural style, he doesn't own it, any more than Little Richard owns Rock and Roll because he invented it. Little Richard is rich because he plays Rock and Roll so well, but anyone can play music in that style without paying royalties to Little Richard.

Many times along this road we thought we might be very rich; there was certainly potential for great wealth. We owned unregistered stock worth $40 million at one point, valued at the price investors actually paid. Then when Multiflow went under, our stock was worthless since all the company assets, including technology licenses, went to pay its debts. There was also a question then of whether Multiflow's creditors would go after our personal assets, impoverishing us, even though Josh had never personally guaranteed the debt. None of that happened, though; we didn't get rich, but we didn't end up in financial ruin.

One person did become rich because of Multiflow, but it was someone who never worked there. Steve Wood had been a graduate student at Yale with many of the first Multiflow employees but had left Yale in 1983 to join a software start-up in the northwest. When Multiflow began, all his friends wanted Steve to work with them. They told him what fun they'd have working on Josh's technology, developing a product that would change the world. His friends had no respect for what Steve was doing—not only software, but personal computing software that was nowhere near the glamorous scientific computing world. They thought his job was beneath him and urged him to join them, doing something really important.

Multiflow made Steve an offer, a better offer than to any of the other engineers: $45,000 salary plus relocation benefits and 22,000 shares of stock. Steve was sorely tempted but he really liked his job. His boss wanted him to stay and offered him a large amount of unregistered stock as an inducement. His boss said that someday this company, Microsoft, would go public and Steve's stock would be worth something. Steve stayed at Microsoft—and it happened just as Bill Gates said it would.

We didn't get rich, but Multiflow made Josh's scientific reputation and also his reputation for recognizing talent and putting together fabulous technical teams. It also made the reputations of virtually all the engineers who worked there. There was a guy who started work the week

Multiflow went under who benefited from its aura—he got a job right away, burnished by being chosen by Multiflow.

VLIW technology also succeeded, even though Multiflow failed as a company. No longer an unknown technology, VLIW now gets nearly a million Google hits at last count. It did not change all scientific computers as Josh and his colleagues thought it should but, through Multiflow licensing agreements and independent development efforts, it has spread throughout the technical community. In 2000, Josh's group at HP Labs developed a VLIW processor with STMicroelectronics, one of the world's largest manufacturers of semiconductors. As of 2012, ST has sold chips with over 500 million of these processors to manufacturers for use in digital video, and HP uses the processor extensively in its printers. In addition, VLIW technology is now used industry-wide as embedded processors in printers, smartphones, computer graphics chips, cable boxes, cell base stations, GPS devices and DVRs. As a result, there is something with VLIW technology in almost every home in the developed world.

THE EUREKA MOMENT

On the Wednesday before Thanksgiving, 1978, Josh was working on his doctoral thesis and waiting for me to come home from my office in New York City. He was in the public library near our home in Teaneck, New Jersey, and when I got home, he, I and our eleven-month-old son, Davey, would drive to Boston to spend the holiday with my brother and sister-in-law.

Josh was a graduate student in computer science at NYU's Courant Institute, and for several years he had worked on a faculty project to emulate the department's supercomputer, a CDC 6600, creating a handmade computer called PUMA. Now he was working on the hardest problem he found on this project, one he hoped to turn into his thesis.

Josh had been worrying at this problem for months and was just starting to see it clearly. Because I was late getting home that Wednesday before Thanksgiving, Josh had extra time in the Teaneck library to work on his thesis, extra time to think deeply, to get really involved—to have his eureka moment.

* * *

In 1978, Josh was 32, older than most computer science graduate students. His life had been less orderly than theirs, and his family background and personal history were also different. Unlike him, many of his fellow students came from upper middle class backgrounds and progressed from college to graduate school with a firm eye on how they would spend their careers. Because Josh was different, his worldview was too. He had an outsider's perspective that shaped his approach to science, helping him to look at the world in unique ways.

His parents grew up poor in New York City, each the oldest of large families. Harry, his father, was not quite seventeen when Josh was born, six months after his parents were married; Sue, his mother, was eighteen: they had only $5 between them when Josh was born. Sue dropped out of high school, but Harry graduated from the High School of Aeronautical Trades, his young family living with his parents in the Bronx while he finished high school. Harry wanted a technical career but, because he had a

**Josh as an infant with his teenaged parents,
Harry and Sue**

family to support, he took a job at Howard Clothes, a men's clothing chain, after he graduated from high school.

Josh's early years were spent in New York City, close to both his parents' families. Between them, his parents had eight brothers and sisters who were still very young themselves, more like Josh's brothers and sisters than his aunts and uncles. For many years, he was the only grandchild, everyone's pet, much fussed over, the only small child at the frequent gatherings of these two large extended families.

His parents often took him to Van Cortlandt Park where the Turkish Sephardic community, Sue's family and all their friends, had large parties that lasted all weekend. There was Turkish music, the men danced and there were bonfires where they roasted shish-kebab. Josh's grandfather, Isaac Cohen, played the Turkish drum at these parties and also at Turkish night clubs all over New York. In addition to drumming, Isaac worked as a foreman in a garment factory. He had been a merchant seaman who

Mollie and Isaac Cohen, Josh's grandparents, in a Turkish night club in New York during the 1950s

jumped ship, immigrating illegally to the US in the early 1920s. Mollie Cohen, Josh's grandmother, also immigrated from Turkey, legally coming through Ellis Island.

Before Josh was born, the Cohen family had terribly disruptive problems: drunkenness, abuse and extreme poverty. Sue and her brothers and sisters all spent time in different foster homes, going back to the family when Mollie thought she could care for them. As teenagers, Sue and both her sisters married men as unlike their father as possible, spending their lives in long-term marriages to very stable men. Despite her difficult family, or maybe because of it, Sue was a wonderful mother—loving and warm—fiercely protective of Josh, her only child.

Josh's paternal grandparents, the Fishers, whom he lived with, were not part of the colorful weekend Sephardic gatherings; they were not Sephardic, and their families had been in the United States for generations. Josh loved his Fisher grandparents, particularly his grandfather, who was the grandfather every boy wants, taking him to baseball games and to watch trains. But the joy of those weekend Sephardic parties—the color, the camaraderie among the men, the music and the dancing—stayed with him always, a vivid reminder of his Sephardic heritage.

When Josh was six, his family moved from New York to Syracuse, and he was abruptly torn from the warmth of these family gatherings. His parents had wanted to move out of the city, but he hated leaving. Josh felt wrenched from most of what he loved, even though his Aunt Betty—Sue's teen-aged sister—moved with them. He missed his other aunts, his uncles and his grandparents; this large family gave him such a strong sense of who he was.

But the move to Syracuse was only the start of Josh's troubles: in school, he found that he couldn't do what his new world expected him to do. He was different from his new classmates, spoke differently and knew different things but, mostly, he couldn't pay attention in class or sit still and do his work.

It was obvious that Josh was smart, but he just didn't fit in. He taught himself to read very early, at age four, but in class his thoughts wandered off, no matter how hard he tried to stay focused. By the time he tuned in again, the class was doing something else and he was lost. He could always figure out math but he was very slow since he never memorized the multiplication or addition tables. When worksheets were handed out in class, he would do the first few problems correctly, then become distracted and daydream, finally handing in his paper with only those first few problems done. He talked incessantly to the kids around him or daydreamed, sometimes seeming absent, sometimes doing many things at once, going from subject to subject, never doing what he was supposed to do.

It never occurred to Josh to ask for help from his teachers; he knew what he was supposed to do—sit down and do his work. But his teachers probably couldn't have helped him anyway. Understanding of this problem, Josh's different learning style, now known as Attention Deficit Disorder, was many years in the future. These days, educators can make accommodations for ADD kids to learn but, in the 1950s and 1960s, they didn't even understand learning disabilities far more severe than what Josh was coping with. And, so, he struggled alone.

Josh's parents were at their wits' end, and they, too, didn't have any idea how to help him. Sue suffered from lapses of attention herself and, being angry at herself, was even angrier at Josh. She couldn't manage her own learning problems, and she didn't know how to help her son. Harry didn't know either, but his approach was more methodical. When he saw an illegible math paper, he spent his own vacation time, Josh's spring vacation, sitting with him while he wrote numbers over and over again until they became neater.

Josh willingly did what his father said. He was miserable in school and wanted to make his life better. Unfortunately, though, while he could concentrate with his father sitting there watching him, that was as far as it went. Harry's efforts helped with legibility but the larger problem remained: Josh's inability to pay attention in class or do homework by himself.

His classmates and even some of the teachers ridiculed him. In first grade he was sent back to kindergarten for a day as punishment, that being where the teacher said he belonged. He got report cards that said "Joseph could do so much better."

In junior high school and beyond, it only got worse because now Josh had to do homework. He wanted to do it and intended to do it but at home he couldn't get himself to sit down and start. Instead he would read, listen to baseball games, listen to music, invent games and play them by himself or watch television. Sometimes a subject would catch his interest—chess, baseball, cars or music—and he delved into it with laser-like focus, enjoying it, learning a lot, even though it called him away from his studies; none of his avocational studying seemed to fit with the classes he was taking. He could focus on his other interests but, undisciplined, he could not focus on his work.

The undone homework embarrassed and humiliated him. He wanted so much to do what he was supposed to do, but couldn't find a way; nothing he tried got him to sit down. Detention at school didn't work, either; he could daydream for any amount of time. Josh was miserable, his only respite coming in summers when he played chess at the Syracuse Chess Club and organized baseball games among his neighborhood friends who didn't know about his humiliations at school.

Many of Josh's teachers were angry at him, seeing his undone homework as an act of will rather than a problem he had little control over. Even Josh saw his learning style as willful, since he could work when he was frightened badly enough. He always failed language classes—German, Spanish and Russian—because he hadn't memorized vocabulary. But in his other classes he had enough background that when the threat of failure frightened him enough, he could hand in reports on books he hadn't read or learn just enough to squeak by on exams. Since he was so smart, his last minute catch-up often made him excel at math, a subject many people found difficult, and when his teachers saw what he could do, they were even angrier.

This made school a horror because anyone was liable to be angry at him and ambushes were everywhere. When he organized the high school chess club and the county chess league, a teacher he didn't know stopped him in the hall.

"Hey, I know you," the teacher said, angrily. "You're that kid, the one who organized the chess league, but can't be bothered to do his homework."

Despite all this, there was no question of Josh's dropping out of school. Everyone in Josh's family told him how smart he was—and education mattered to them. Sue regretted not finishing high school and Harry wished he had gone to college. If Josh had stopped his schooling, he would have disappointed his parents and his entire extended family whom he loved so much. Also, despite how awful school was for him, Josh loved to learn. The time he spent researching arcane subjects was some of his happiest, and he knew that school was the key to learning. If only he behaved better, he thought, he could learn the way he wanted to.

Josh's family expected that he would go to college and because he was persuasive, they thought that he would someday be a lawyer. At family weddings, Passover, and Rosh Hashanah, the large family fussed over him, teased him about talking too much and about trying to convince anyone who would listen to agree to his viewpoint on any issue. They loved him, knew he was a good kid and believed that he could do anything in the world. They saw him in a courtroom, swaying a jury, selling them on his way of thinking.

But Josh's family didn't know what was involved in being a lawyer, didn't understand the studying necessary to become one. They didn't have the background. Only one person in the family, Harry's brother Sam, had been to college; most of the rest of the family worked in sales—his parents sold clothes and his aunts, uncles and his aunts' husbands sold cameras, aluminum siding, advertising space, and real estate. They only knew what they saw on television and that Josh was fully as smart and persuasive as Perry Mason.

And Josh was persuasive, from his earliest years, and he learned it mostly from his mother. Sue shared Josh's ADD personality, perhaps inheriting it along with others in her family. She was the buyer and manager of lingerie for a department store, the creativity and gregariousness that went along with the distractibility leading to her success. She couldn't sit down and study, but she was very good at selling.

Sales was Sue's real passion and at the family dinner table she taught it to Josh. It was usually just the two of them, since Josh was an only child and Harry often had to work late, so the lessons were intense. Harry had strong opinions about selling but, unlike Sue, when he sold clothes he used the aura of authority he projected, rather than persuasion.

Josh worked in sales, too, growing up, at Howard Clothes; he also sold magazine subscriptions, greeting cards and newspapers, and hot dogs at sports events. Between high school and college, he traveled through the South as part of a group of young salesmen putting on promotional events: "Pony Day" give-aways at minor league baseball games, selling advertising as they went. He was good a it, too; his sales technique combining his mother's persuasive abilities with his father's aura of authority, making him a leader.

He liked selling, seeing it as a way to make money that he could be good at, much easier than his struggles with school. It provided free range for his creativity and an outlet for his talkativeness, his need to convince others to see his viewpoint. And he liked the excitement and the sense of mastery it gave him. He worked hard to perfect the craft, applying himself as he was not able to in school; the qualities that were weaknesses in school—his expansiveness and ability to go from subject to subject—became strengths in salesmanship.

Josh's favorite salesperson was the Veg-O-Matic man who sold food processors at the New York State Fair. Every year he spent hours watching him capture the audience, making it all look so easy, slicing and dicing, convincing the customers that they could do it too if only they bought the expensive machine and took it home. As Josh watched, he never wanted to buy the machine; he had no interest in slicing or dicing. He was interested in how the salesman swayed the audience. Admiring the combination of skill and patter, he watched to see how it was done.

When it was time to apply to college, Josh knew where he wanted to go; he had always wanted to return to New

York. His family was there and so was his heart. He forced himself to get decent grades first semester of his senior year, panicked that he would be left behind. And that, along with spectacular SATs, got him in. In 1964, he moved back to New York City to go to NYU.

Josh started college as a pre-law freshman, wanting to fulfill his family's expectations, but he ran into trouble. The learning style that plagued him, his constant distraction and difficulty concentrating, caught up with him and made it very hard for him in classes that he didn't find fascinating. College was more complex than high school, too, where basic knowledge had enabled a quick catch-up at the end. He couldn't do that in college, and failed several classes.

Upset and on the verge of flunking out, Josh considered dropping out of college. He spent many anguished days with his Uncle Sam, the one college graduate in the family, trying to figure out if there was any way for him to stay in school. He decided to take easy classes his second semester to buy time so that he could decide what to do. Because he liked math in high school, one of the easy classes he took was calculus. To Josh's surprise, he loved calculus, and it caught his interest so much that he was able to work on his own, to sit down and concentrate, giving him his first real success in school. He changed his major to math, and really took hold.

I met Josh during the summer of 1965, between our freshman and sophomore years of college. We met at the Times Square restaurant where we both had jobs; I was a waitress and he was a cashier. I was immediately attracted to his lively imagination, his unique view of the world, and to his dark good looks from his Sephardic ancestors. After our first few dates, Josh and I became inseparable. We married a year and a half after we met, in the middle of our junior years in college.

I had never met anyone with so many real interests, such a dazzling intellectual life or such a wonderful sense of fun. Besides mathematics, Josh cared about electronics, music of all kinds, sports of all kinds, local and national politics, cars, economics—the list went on and on—and he had so much to say, so many opinions about everything. His world seemed so much richer than the world I lived in and he enjoyed it all so much. When we looked at the same thing, Josh would see twice as much as I did, and so much of it was fascinating. The contrast with my WASP relatives and the boys I was used to going out with was breathtaking, and I was enthralled.

Josh and me in 1967 on the roof of
our building, E 11th St, New York City

I was amazed by how excited Josh was by mathematics, how devoted he was to the idea that this was the way he would spend his life. He often closed himself in the bathroom of our one room apartment at night, not wanting to wake me, but complaining about the excessive heat coming from the bathroom riser pipe distracting him from his subject. He worked all night, expansively thinking he had made a brilliant discovery, something fundamental in mathematics that would insure his reputation as a mathematician. By the morning, he had usually learned that his insight was wrong or that it was something others had previously worked through, but his love of mathematics stayed strong.

After college, Josh began a Ph.D. program at McGill University in Montreal, but graduate mathematics was a shock, far more complex than his undergraduate classes. He had always understood mathematics without effort, but now he had to work very hard. He loved the subject and had done well in college; he wanted to do well in graduate school, too. He didn't understand why he couldn't buckle down and study at McGill, why the learning style which had tortured him during his high school years had come back to paralyze him.

As a mathematics graduate student Josh had to do a lot of literature searches, laborious in the pre-internet age and especially so in math, an ancient subject with a long history to look through. When he started a search, he would begin normally enough but then he would put down his papers, wander away, start something else, or take a nap.

I watched all this with alarm; I couldn't understand what was happening. Josh was smart, talented and capable, yet he wasn't working. I was more confused than angry, not knowing what to make of it. I had heard about Josh's high school troubles but since I hadn't been there, I really didn't understand them. Now I saw him wanting desperately to work, yet not doing it. It looked to me like something he could control yet as I watched him struggle, I could see that he couldn't. Since I knew Josh was a steady reliable person, it made no sense to me, and I felt terrible about the pain he was going through.

Josh stuck it out for a full year, trying to work at the graduate program he had set his heart on. He did research, getting results he was happy with, but the studying was too much for him. Painfully, he decided to leave McGill.

Deeply disappointed, with his dreams of becoming a mathematician blocked, Josh didn't know what to do next. Searching for a way to stay in that world, he decided to become a computer programmer. Wanting to get as far away as possible from his thwarted ambitions, he decided that we should move to Los Angeles. We picked up everything, including our cats, and drove out to California. We settled into an apartment and both took temporary jobs. But in the late 1960s, many people were drifting in and out of Los Angeles and employers distrusted people who had just moved there. Josh had no luck finding permanent work, not even with his credentials in math and, three months later, we packed up our cats and drove back across the country.

In New York, it took Josh years to find his calling. He tried again in graduate mathematics, starting PhD programs first at Yeshiva University and then at NYU, both as a student of our friend Martin Davis. While in these programs, wanting to start an academic career, Josh taught math at colleges all over the New York area: Hunter College, NYU, Brooklyn College, Bronx Community College and Queensboro Community College, sometimes driving across New York City and back several times a day.

Josh teaching at Brooklyn College, 1970

He tried hard, but in his new graduate programs, Josh had the same problems he had at McGill, the same inability to concentrate, to sit down and study or do literature searches. When he didn't do well enough on his NYU PhD qualifying exams, he decided that an academic career in mathematics was not in his future. He'd gotten the best shot anyone could give him and it hadn't worked. If he couldn't make it as Martin's student, then he simply wasn't going to make it. Josh didn't know what to do.

When he left school again he repaired washing machines, drove a taxi, worked for a real estate developer, and sold Oriental rugs—a long series of jobs he held for three months each, each time thinking that this job, finally, would be the one he would spend his life at. He started with the highest hopes but criticism from a boss, embarrassment over his own imperfections on the job, the irritations and irrationalities of imperfect co-workers and working conditions would all trip him up. The weight of constant unfulfilled obligations oppressed him. He felt like he wasn't performing the way he wanted, doing the job the way he or anyone else wanted, that he was letting everyone down. He was serious about every one of these jobs, yet left quickly when they didn't work out, going on to the next job where he thought that, this time, he would find a place where he could show his true worth.

All this turmoil was hard on Josh, and it was hard on me, too. I loved him and was truly prepared to encourage anything he could be happy at. He could be a college professor, fix air conditioners or drive a cab—it was all fine with me. But I wondered if Josh would ever find what he wanted and I needed more stability. There had been so many changes in the past few years that I was beginning to despair, getting to the breaking point, worrying about what would happen to us.

Each time, when Josh told me that his new job would be his career, I believed him. Then, when he left it, I was crushed, scrambling to figure out how we would live our lives. After a while, though, I couldn't bear to have my hopes crushed each time a new career didn't work out. The roller coaster was too much for me, and I asked him not to talk about his future. I couldn't stand to think about it any more. When Josh started talking about moving to Tennessee where we had spent a happy summer, uprooting us again, I thought about staying in New York without him.

But then something wonderful happened. For years, through our the tumultuous changes, I had been telling Josh that the problems he was having were coming from inside himself, not from the jobs he had tried and rejected. Martin told him the same thing, with greater authority, since he was a mathematician, a revered being in Josh's mind. Finally, at the end of his rope, Josh started to believe it, to believe his problems were coming from inside himself.

I had had a good experience with a psychiatrist when my parents divorced, but no one in Josh's family or anyone else he knew had ever tried psychotherapy. It was foreign to him. He was desperate, though, and didn't know where else to turn.

He went to the Psychology section of the Kingsbridge public library near our home in the Bronx and started reading. He began with the first book in the section and when he got to those by Karen Horney, way beyond Freud, he recognized himself. He started seeing a psychiatrist at the Karen Horney Institute in New York three days a week and applied himself to psychoanalysis the way he had to mathematics in college.

As he started psychoanalysis, Josh started another new job—teaching mathematics at a private high school. Three months after an enthusiastic start, like clockwork, he began thinking he should quit, running from everything that wasn't perfect.

But psychoanalysis was changing him. At one point, he told his analyst he "should" do a particular thing to improve himself, something desirable but extraneous, like learning to speak Spanish.

"Why?" she asked.

He had no answer and, somehow, it had never occurred to him to ask the question. He thought he was required to do all sorts of things, that everyone was, that it was only his own inadequacies preventing him from doing all the things he "should." He saw then how driven he was, how the weight of obligation oppressed him. He felt he needed to do everything perfectly, from the smallest day-to-day tasks to the most important career-related work. No wonder he found life so hard. No wonder he kept running away.

Very quickly, Josh started feeling happier, less guilty when he didn't do things perfectly, less like he was letting everyone down. He realized that he had been so hard on himself, so critical, that he hadn't been able to stand criticism from anyone else. He also hadn't been able appreciate his strengths. He began to be easier on himself, to relax and to enjoy his life. His life—and my life with it—got better, Josh's anguish no longer coloring everything we did. I thought it was a miracle as I watched the man I fell in love with in college emerge from his despair.

Because it was 1973, and not the 1990s when ADD was discovered, Josh's psychoanalysis did not address his learning style. That didn't go away, but psychoanalysis taught him to live with it, even to understand some of its benefits. He also learned to be sympathetic with himself when he didn't live up to his high standards, to tame some of his perfectionism.

The combination of that perfectionism, which came from his father and the ADD, which came from his mother, was what had made his life so difficult: he couldn't get himself to do what he wanted, then he blamed himself for not living up to his standards. These traits continued inside him, but psychoanalysis taught him to ease up—and it was enough. It allowed him to do what he wanted to do, accomplishing more, without the constant weight of responsibility. His world got lighter.

* * *

Josh stayed at his high school teaching job and, without our realizing it, the whole school year slipped by. He had always loved teaching, and been good at it, since it is so similar to sales, and he found he really liked what he was doing. With psychoanalysis, he was putting less pressure on himself, and he found life carefree. He decided that he could be happy as a high school teacher. Then, wanting to teach the smartest students, Josh began another doctoral program at NYU, this one in mathematics education. With his life easier, he was able to tame his learning style and apply himself to his classes. We both began to look ahead to a normal life, without all the tumult of the last few years. It looked as though Josh's life was set to go on an even keel, that he could relax into his life as a teacher.

All this changed, though, and made a dramatic turn, when Josh took a computer architecture class. The legendary mathematician and computer scientist Jack Schwartz spoke at one class meeting and Josh's world opened up. Listening to Jack's lyrical description of computer architecture, the logical structure of the computer, Josh felt the same excitement he felt as an undergraduate studying math. Suddenly he was understanding issues that had always bothered him, for instance, how does a computer start from a stand-still? He remembered that thrill, the thrill of scientific discovery, something that was missing from his life as a high school teacher, and he knew he wanted it back. He realized he could have that thrill again, in computer science, a more collaborative science than mathematics had been, a new science with less literature to search, a new field with significant discoveries still to be made.

Josh asked Jack to suggest a faculty project for him to work on, and Jack suggested PUMA, which was designing an emulator for the department's supercomputer, the CDC 6600, in the computer science department. When Josh started working on PUMA, he realized that this, really, was what he wanted. He switched to a graduate program in computer science and never looked back.

* * *

In the Teaneck library in 1978, that Wednesday before Thanksgiving, three years after hearing Jack Schwartz' computer architecture lecture, Josh considered his thesis problem. His different learning style now worked for him, not against him, taking him into creative flights of fancy in unconventional directions as he worked through his ideas. He had passed both his written and oral qualifying exams and now wanted to finish his thesis as soon as he could.

PUMA, the computer emulator designed by his advisor, was controlled by microcode—burned-in instructions at the lowest level of the computer, a program running all the time. The microcode was horizontal; that is, many of the instructions were executed together, in parallel, so that the computer would run faster. But the horizontal code needed to be handwritten, a very difficult job. It was like a thousand piece jigsaw puzzle; when something changes, it throws everything else off. You couldn't just shoehorn in a solution; you had to take it all apart and start again.

For Josh's thesis, he wanted to find a way to automatically create horizontal microcode from sequential microcode: that is, for the computer to take the programmer's sequential code, with all its branches, and transform it automatically into horizontal code. This was the hardest problem he had found working on PUMA.

When Josh had researched his problem, he found that there were no good solutions. Few other computer scientists had considered it, and those that had hadn't gotten very far. This was partly because many of them were hardware engineers who proposed ineffective or impractical solutions which hadn't worked well enough because rearranging instructions is a software problem that hardware engineers didn't have the background to solve.

Josh realized early on that what he was doing was a little like a field of applied mathematics, "job shop scheduling," part of operations research. This was used by manufacturers to figure out the most efficient way of scheduling materials and machines to produce products, that is, which activities could be done at the same time in a factory. He could apply this technique to a computer program when code was sequential and looked like a manufacturing assembly line; he just didn't know how to handle branches in his code—something unique to computer programs. Most scientists who had worked on Josh's problem also had no idea how to handle branches, and this was important since they occurred every five to eight instructions. Their technique was to look at small sections of code and try to improve each one.

That day, looking at his problem from a computer science perspective, Josh suddenly saw it in a new way—a bigger picture, one rooted in his different way of looking at life, not as focused on the component parts. With a flash of insight, he realized that if he were hand coding, he wouldn't be looking at small sections of code, he would look at the whole program. And he thought he could write software that would do just that: look at the whole program, not just a small section, looking at it the way he would if he were doing the coding by hand. As it looked at the code, the program could make a guess about the most likely path the code would take through the branches.

After the computer had that first path, it could look at it and find parallelism along the way, adding code to compensate if the guess was wrong. After that first guess, the computer could do it again, finding parallelism along the next path, fixing the guesses with more compensation code. Then it could look at the rest of the code and find parallelism the same way, again and again, following the same process until it had looked at all the code. This was a lot like the way Josh would do it if he were hand coding. And he thought that if the program he wrote to do this worked, it would be a real breakthrough, automatically speeding up the computer without laborious hand coding.

This flash of insight was Josh's eureka moment. When he first saw it, he saw a fully formed idea, untested, with missing details, but complete. The idea stunned him. It was a new idea and, as he looked at it, Josh was convinced that it could work; if it did, it would not only make hand parallelizing unnecessary, but it would produce amazingly fast code.

* * *

In the Teaneck library, Josh quickly wrote up the outline of his idea, finishing before I got home from work. I had been delayed long enough for him to have his Eureka moment, but he realized that he would have to spend a lot of his Thanksgiving in Boston working to see if his idea was as promising as he thought.

We drove to Boston through the heavy holiday traffic, Josh quiet as he drove, working his idea out in his mind, resisting all my attempts at conversation. He drove safely, though, using his ability to do many things at once. When we got to Boston, he disappeared, after greeting our family; he needed to write up the thoughts he had been working on during our drive.

The next morning, Thanksgiving, and for the rest of the weekend, Josh got up before dawn, very cold, grumbling about his brother-in-law's old, drafty house that was so hard to heat. He huddled in the living room, the warmest room in the house, working on his idea, laser focused in the way he could be when an idea grabbed his attention.

I had seen Josh excited about problems before, from our earliest days together when he was studying mathematics as an undergraduate. But this time, it seemed different. As I watched him, he seemed more intent, more certain that he had a hold of something important. And he worked steadily—all weekend looking for the flaw that would tell him that he was on the wrong track. But he didn't find anything wrong.

When we got home from Boston, Josh continued working, feverishly, for the weeks and months that followed. He became more and more convinced that his idea would work, that he could make a significant contribution to computer science. Larger implications flashed through his mind. He had been thrilled in the Teaneck library to think that he might have solved a small, difficult programming problem; now he began to think that his technique could be used with all horizontal code. If horizontal code could be generated automatically, more machines could be built to use it, machines with simpler, less expensive hardware since all they would need to do would be to follow instructions from the software.

Looking at a diagram of a test program, Josh drew a line around the instructions in the path the computer might take to find parallelism. The shape was amoeba-like, ghostly, since it included instructions from several branches. Josh thought of this shape as a "trace," after the usual name for the path through the code and, reminiscent of job shop scheduling, he called his technique "trace scheduling."

* * *

By early 1979, Josh was sure enough that he would finish his PhD that he began to look for a tenure track faculty job in computer science for the following September. He confined his search to the New York metropolitan area because I had a job I loved in midtown Manhattan, working in product development at the

Equitable. Ahead of his time in many ways, he saw nothing wrong with restricting his job search for my sake.

My job was important to me and I told people that it wasn't so bad that Josh was only interviewing at Yale and Princeton and everything in between but, really, I was torn. I had grown up in a world where women's work was less important than men's and for years I had followed Josh. But he was no longer the conflicted, confused young man of ten years earlier who had taken us from New York to Montreal, then to California and back again. Josh had matured with the accomplishments of the last few years and calmed down. He didn't want me to have to leave my job. He had what he wanted, success at work he loved, and he wanted me to have it, too. Josh's easy acceptance and his good cheer made it easier for me, and I tried not to feel guilty.

Applying for faculty jobs as a new PhD involved giving a talk on your research and, at all the universities he visited, Josh had a compelling new software technique to talk about, trace scheduling. Like the Veg-O-Matic man of his youth, he painted dramatic pictures when he spoke; these were pictures of how trace scheduling could change computing and his audience was captivated. After looking at most of the universities in the New York metropolitan area, Josh liked the Yale department best and accepted the job they offered.

He had been working hard, but now with a deadline ahead, he seemed to double his pace, writing furiously to finish his thesis in time. He wrote up his work, did experiments to test traditional job shop scheduling algorithms in relation to trace scheduling, and ran simulations of what it might accomplish and ways it might go faster using resource allocation. He also described trace scheduling algorithmically so that it could be implemented, but when he didn't implement it himself, not being able to afford the years needed to do it, Jack Schwartz threatened to hold up his degree.

Jack was famous for graduate students whose thesis work went into a second decade, but he was not Josh's advisor. That was Ralph Grishman, the PUMA principal investigator, and Ralph thought Josh had done all he needed. He had a job at Yale calling to him, so Jack relented and Josh got his degree, moving on to Yale.

YALE

The Yale campus is beautiful with its Neogothic buildings and large open green spaces, very different from urban NYU. The buildings on Old Campus have leaded windows and chandeliers hanging from soaring ceilings. Beinecke Library, filled with rare books, is made of glowing, translucent marble and, even with its small size, is one of the most valuable buildings in the country because of the material it is made from. In 1979, the NYU downtown campus didn't have a gym; at Yale, the gym looked like a European cathedral. History and the legacy of famous graduates are everywhere—as is evidence of wealth and patrician WASP culture.

When I was an undergraduate at Barnard, Josh resisted going to events at Columbia, hostile to anything Ivy League. The atmosphere of understated elegance combined with genteel shabbiness was different from anything he understood, different from any of his family's experience. He thought it was pretentious and empty and avoided Columbia, sticking to NYU; in 1979, nothing Ivy League had been part of our lives for many years.

But when Josh began looking for a job as a new PhD, he couldn't afford to pay attention to his prejudices. His years in psychoanalysis had settled him down; he was no longer so threatened by such a foreign environment and warily interviewed at Princeton—and at Columbia, too. Yale seemed too far away, but Jack Schwartz heard that their Computer Science Department was looking for someone in

31

computer architecture and encouraged him to apply. Looking at a map, we thought we could do it. How Josh would feel in a job at an Ivy League school was a different question.

But Jack reassured Josh, telling him that Alan Perlis, the Yale Computer Science Chair, had built a great department where he could be happy; he wouldn't find any pretension there. Perlis was a computer science pioneer, involved in the early development of modern computers, winner of the first Turing Award. Because Alan was in systems, the part of the field where computer architecture fit, it was important at Yale. Jack thought it would be a good match.

Even with those good words, Josh was apprehensive as he approached his Yale interview, not knowing what to expect.

"Don't let the ivy snow you," our friend Martin told him as he set out. Martin had gotten his PhD at Princeton and shared Josh's ambivalence about the Ivy League.

Josh liked Alan Perlis right away, and he was delighted by an enthusiastic reception from the bright young faculty and from graduate students smarter than any he had ever seen. Everyone at Yale was wildly enthusiastic about their work and it was contagious. Their excitement about their academic projects was different from anything Josh had found at his other interviews and he wanted to be part of it.

On the train trip going home, Josh sat next to Geoff Lowney, a graduate student who lived in New York City. He liked Geoff and liked the atmosphere he described at Yale of free-wheeling, creative building. Josh was attracted to it, but a little frightened because it made NYU seem stodgy by comparison.

* * *

After Josh accepted the job at Yale, we decided to move half way along the eighty mile distance from New York to New Haven, thinking this would prevent either of us from having a crippling commute. This brought us to Fairfield County, CT, a far more expensive place than Teaneck.

We bought the cheapest house in Darien, CT, perched at the edge of Interstate 95, with the Metro North train just across the highway. We had a small grocery store next door to us and a pediatrician's office across the intersection. It was not as nice as our home in Teaneck and not nearly as nice as a home we could buy near New Haven, but I had a job I loved, and Josh was looking forward to Yale. Our three hour daily commutes seemed worth it to both of us. I was fully signed on for this new life.

That fall, Josh found, to his dismay, that many of the young faculty members who lit up his interview the previous spring had left. He felt blindsided, even though he should have known this might happen. There was a lot of job-hopping then, with limitless opportunities for computer scientists; everyone knew that losing people was a danger. At his Princeton interview, Josh had asked if anyone was leaving the department and had gotten cagey answers, but he hadn't asked at Yale. The upshot was that Josh entered a department with a near vacuum in systems.

But even though most of the systems faculty was gone, Alan Perlis was still there. He was not as dynamic as he once was, with advancing multiple sclerosis diminishing his abilities, but his intellectual capacity was as strong as ever. He was the same outgoing, charming leader who started the Computer Science Department at Carnegie Tech and had been president of the computer professional society, the ACM. He was weakened, in a wheel chair and without any projects of his own, but he was an easy-going, informal person.

Because of Perlis and the department he created, the faculty departures mattered less than Josh feared. The graduate students were still there, and so was the culture; Alan's powerful eco-system had critical mass, a dynamic so big that it dominated the department. It was so entrenched that a few departures, even important ones, couldn't diminish it.

Perlis became Josh's teacher and his closest colleague, teaching him the philosophy of programming and systems building as a real art, not simply as a means to an end. Josh sought him out because he liked talking to him; in his office, in the halls, the conversation always turned to systems research. Perlis never thought conventionally. He thoughts ranged across all of computer science and how to teach it, too; he once told Josh that programmers needed classes in how to read programs before they tried to write them. A lot of things he said sounded crazy, really outrageous, and sometimes they actually were crazy. It was hard to tell the difference. But Josh would realize, over and over again, three hours after talking to Perlis, that he had just heard something of stunning brilliance.

Because of Alan Perlis, research while building real things became the theme of Josh's career. Alan taught him that exploring an idea while doing something practical creates a far more powerful result than considering the idea on its own. Many scientists don't think of building as science but in Perlis' radical view, you learn much more and do better science when you can't wish away reality, when it is a force that you have to push against.

This principle became part of Josh and he applied it to everything. When it was his turn to do graduate admissions at Yale, it was the first year that students were allowed to leave China after the Cultural Revolution, and he was faced with twenty identically glowing applications from

34

institutions he had never heard of and had no way to judge. Since the Chinese knew about Yale from its early missionary connection, the department expected to see these applications increase and couldn't ignore them. Josh thought he should choose one student to admit, and see how he did. But which student should he let into Yale?

Josh chose Kai Li, and it was because Kai was a builder. His personal admissions statement described the working television he had built from vacuum tubes he had scavenged from junk yards in a ruined China. Josh thought Kai must be special, not to mention ingenious, to build something himself under such difficult circumstances and to show such pride in it. On Josh's recommendation, Yale admitted Kai, and he did well. He became a student of Alan Perlis, Alan's last student, and later a chaired professor and prodigious researcher in the Computer Science Department at Princeton.

Years later, when our son Dave was fourteen, Kai came to dinner at our home in Boston. He told us stories of his life during the Cultural Revolution when he was Dave's age, virtually homeless, roaming China by train with his younger brother. His father had been a professor at a medical school and academics were a particular target of the revolutionaries.

As Kai talked, I sat there listening, spell-bound, and tears came to my eyes as I imagined Dave in those horrible circumstances. Kai told us that when the Chinese government put him to work, he was assigned to a steel plant, a hellish place where his job was to tilt and pour a huge container of molten steel. To relieve the boredom, he found a few books and taught himself graduate level physics. Then, when the turmoil was winding down and China realized it needed educated citizens, Kai was chosen to study computer science as an undergraduate, assigned to the subject at random. He told us he could just as easily have been chosen to study economics or medicine: he had no choice. He credited Josh with getting him out of China, letting him bring his family over, enabling him to make a life in America.

* * *

When he first got to Yale, Josh found the students intimidating, brilliant and far more roundly educated than students at NYU. Yalies knew so much, and they could all write so well, even the computer science graduate students. He felt out of place, thinking all the students and faculty were better educated than he was—it scared him.

Many nights Josh came home from work worried about his future, describing his fears to me at the dinner table. I understood that Josh's education had been different, but I never agreed with him. I thought he was brilliant, and it seemed to me that anything he lacked in breadth he more than made up for by his creativity and depth. I was sure that Josh would find his place, sure that no one he was meeting was smarter than him. My encouragement fell on deaf ears, though, as Josh continued to be anxious, facing people more intellectually adept than any he had ever known.

But before too long he found groups of attentive, enthusiastic students who were eager to learn, students who cared about the compiler and architecture classes he taught his first semester. He relaxed, enjoying his teaching and his research discussions with colleagues and students. He made friends and became part of the department; he started to fit in. And he switched his game from paddleball played on the New York City courts to the more aristocratic game of squash, played in the cathedral-like gym at Yale.

He soon was part of the Computer Science Department's competitive ladder.

Josh's computer architecture class, a joint graduate/undergraduate course, became *the* exciting systems class to take in the Department. Everyone wanted in. And many students who took it became interested in trace scheduling. With Alan not leading any research, Josh ran the only practical systems project in the department. It was a natural for some of the students, especially ideal for a core group of smart systems graduate students who were used to working together. They weren't all part of Josh's project, but they all followed its progress.

The Tools Group, as they called themselves, was a dynamic, fun-loving bunch of students who delighted in building software for the whole department to use. They were the smartest of the smart, and they designed tools for practical use in a spirit of altruism. They built text editors, email programs, and graphics interfaces for the departmental computers, the terminals and the Imagen laser printer, working with macho exuberance because the work was so exciting, so much fun and because they could. If a system couldn't do something, they built a tool to make it do that something, working separately or together, each one writing a module. They, too, had learned from Perlis about building as research, and they delighted in it. It was a great laboratory for these smart, creative people who could reason so imaginatively about computers.

The Tools Group thought Steve Wood was their best builder, but Josh thought it was John Ellis and asked him to be his teaching assistant. The other graduate students were stellar builders, too: Bob Nix, Doug Baldwin, Geoff Lowney, Nat Mishkin, John Ruttenberg, Richard Kelsey, as were undergraduates, Steve Wager, Olin Shivers, Tom Karzes, and Ben Cutler.

Before the internet, before better graphics, before widespread access to powerful computing and applications to do anything you want, long before hacking meant criminal activity, the students delighted in their abilities to make the computer perform. The group played tricks on each other, the undergraduates getting into battles to hack into each other's accounts and the departmental machines. At one point all the error messages from the Imagen printer started "Swine!..."

Calling someone a hacker was a badge of honor in those days, a sign your peers respected you. The best hackers were the most accomplished, the ones everyone looked up to—what everyone wanted to be. None of the Yale students thought they had anything but the purest intent, and they reveled in what they could do.

One morning Josh turned on his terminal to find it suddenly going blazingly fast, much faster than it had gone the day before. A couple of the graduate students had gone into the computer system the night before, adjusted some of the settings and added some routines here and there to speed up the communication time with the terminals. The Systems Administrator, proprietary about the computers, had steam coming out of his ears. He talked about disciplinary action and soon slowed the machine back down. Then a memo appeared, purporting to be from him, describing the horrors of having the machine go fast. It was ironic and gentle but to the point, beautifully written, since the actual authors were Yale students. Ultimately, though, the lure of a faster computer was too much, and the speed-up put in by the Tools Group was restored. A few years later, John O'Donnell became Systems Administrator and had none of these problems. John was in there with the hackers, changing things and fiddling with the systems, making everything go faster.

The students were better builders than Josh was, and he learned from them, trying his hand at projects similar to theirs. When John O'Donnell came to Yale, he hung out with them, too. It was a good group, compatible in outlook and approach, everyone learning together. This was Josh's first exposure to the Zen of Building, the pleasure of systems building for the sheer joy of it. As a graduate student, he had a little of this thrill when he worked on PUMA, but not like at Yale. PUMA had been a pale imitation with very few students; this was the mainstream, the real thing.

I was thrilled when Josh described all this to me, thrilled at his growth and how comfortable he was becoming at Yale. I saw him branching out, learning in ways neither of us had expected, working with people as smart as he was. Josh respected the Tools Group in a way that the other faculty didn't. He valued their ability to do practical work, seeing it as the research technique Perlis had taught him it was. He grew close to the students, seeing them every day. His office was in a remote corridor of the Computer Science Department near most of their offices. There were weekly systems lunches, and they went out together at other times, too. They developed strong bonds, even life-saving ones.

Josh got a reputation as a hero a few years after he arrived at Yale when Geoff Lowney collapsed with a ruptured aneurysm and he rushed across the street to get a doctor.

"Look, there's someone dying over there," Josh said, desperate to get the doctor to go with him when she was reluctant to leave an examining room he had burst into.

Geoff recovered and the doctor, who waited with them until the ambulance came, probably wasn't necessary, but it was a dramatic incident and the students all remembered it.

* * *

Josh and his students worked to implement trace scheduling, the software solution to finding parallelism at the instruction level that Josh had invented for his PhD thesis. As his thinking evolved, it changed from his initial idea that trace scheduling should be used after the programmer's code had been compiled—translated into the computer's own instruction language. John Ruttenberg pointed out that the compiler makes too many decisions while it is working, many of which could undermine its effectiveness. Trace scheduling needed to be part of the compiler, to interact with the rest of that program for it to produce the speed-up they wanted; research now focused on creating a trace scheduling compiler.

And Josh drew his work into a much larger context. He saw trace scheduling as part of a whole new field, coining the term "instruction level parallelism," encompassing all efforts to speed up computing by executing operations in parallel. His creative vision, part of the ADD personality, let him see many things at once, as it had when he invented trace scheduling. Now it led him to expand his work, consolidating it into an entirely new field of study which included his work.

He attracted students, willing workers on his research. As a young faculty member, though, he had not yet figured out how all the pieces went together: the students, the teaching, the research and how it was all paid for. Roger Shank, who became Department Chair after Perlis grew too weak, taught Josh the harsh realities of academic life for a scientist. Research was important, Roger told him, but what really mattered to Josh's career was being awarded research grants. Whether he stayed at Yale depended on it. His students' financial support depended on it. Half his salary and all his summer support depended on it. And since granting agencies only funded scientists who were "visible," Josh had to give talks, as many as he could, and publish papers, spreading his work as far as possible.

"Agencies won't fund you because they like your project," Roger said. "They have to know who you are."

Josh took Roger's advice to heart, understanding that this was his life now and tried to adapt, but the academic star system came as a shock. Josh had assumed that his science would stand on its own; it never occurred to him he had to put himself forward like this, that so much depended on how he presented himself. It put a lot of pressure on him—all a lot more entrepreneurial than he had expected.

And it shocked me too; I didn't know so much was expected of university faculty. I was horrified to find that Josh needed to raise his own research money—and part of his salary—who would have expected such a thing? It didn't go with the dignity I expected in a college professor—especially at Yale.

But Josh had always been persuasive and good at public speaking—like his family, so many of them in sales. He remembered the Veg-O-Matic man of his youth, selling food processors at the New York State Fair, but now he had other role models for selling, ones in the sciences. As an undergraduate he had watched Hans Rademacher, a German number theorist, illustrate points during a talk with wooden props and Grace Murray Hopper, a computer scientist, contrast nanoseconds with microseconds by using wire to show how far an electron could travel in those times. Josh didn't have props to use as they had, but he realized that the showmanship of his youth had a place in science.

And after a while he began traveling, giving talks on trace scheduling at conferences and universities and looking for grants at public agencies. In his quest for research dollars, Josh was impressive as he traveled the country, convincing his colleagues of the value of his research. The National Science Foundation, the Office of Naval Research and the Army Research Office awarded him grants, and Yale won an NSF Centers of Excellence grant largely because of his work. I thought of him as the "scientist who can sell," and his colleagues across the country started to know who he was.

This odyssey took him everywhere and brought him both closer to and farther away from his colleagues. On a puddle jumper going to the Office of Navel Research in Monterey, California, Josh sat next to HT Kung, a senior Carnegie faculty member, who was gracious to Josh as a young researcher, a charming companion on the airplane. But when they got to ONR, Kung realized that Josh was not some scrubini researcher with a promising software technique, as he had thought on the airplane, but someone after the same grant money as he was, trying to take research dollars away from him. When they presented their work at ONR, he put Josh through the most thorough grilling that he had ever had. But he had the research results and got the grant, bringing the money home for Yale.

* * *

During the summer of 1980, his first at Yale, Josh consulted for General Electric, working to adapt trace scheduling to a Floating Point Systems computer, a machine used in GE CT scanners. The FPS hardware was designed for high performance, but was very difficult to program because it was designed to use parallelism determined in advance, creating a nightmare maintaining the CT scanners.

John Lewis, a Yale post-doc about to start work at GE, suggested they consider trace scheduling; the FPS hardware made it a good candidate. If trace scheduling could generate usable code automatically, the FPS system would become a far more practical computer, one that could be used on far more applications, and the CT scanners would go faster and be more reliable.

Josh worked from our home in Darien all summer using a DSL line GE installed in our spare bedroom. He worked slowly, the connection running at only 4800 baud, but he had high hopes. This was the first time anyone had tried to use trace scheduling in a real environment, outside the laboratory. A real implementation—just what Josh had been waiting for. Producing faster CT scan images, cheaper and more reliably was important, practical work.

But the GE project failed. Josh couldn't get enough speed-up to matter. The FPS computer was too fussy to benefit from trace scheduling. Its complicated hardware defeated the efforts to find parallelism, the thing trace scheduling did.

Josh was bitterly disappointed and embarrassed to have failed in his consulting contract. Again, he came to our dinner table in Darien worried about his future, unsure how to go forward, and I sympathized with him. Josh had really expected success, and so had I, expected that his technology would improve the FPS ease of use significantly. We had many bad days, thinking about what this would mean for his career.

But determined not to be defeated by this set-back and to learn from it, Josh began thinking through how to use trace scheduling to advantage. He was convinced that it was a valuable technique; he just hadn't been able to use it effectively yet. He began to think in different directions and to think big.

Machines that found parallelism in the hardware dominated the industry. The FPS machine was different; it was designed to use parallelism found before the code reached the hardware. Josh was convinced this was better, and he was encouraged that the FPS machine had been built to take advantage of the kind of parallelism that his software technique found. This meant that some of the industry appreciated this style.

He learned that there was another computer, the CDC Cyberplus, with hardware also designed for parallelism found before programs were run, designed to compete with the FPS computer. Josh got the architecture manual but again found that the hardware was too fussy, simply too idiosyncratic, to effectively use trace scheduling.

"The hardware guys are never going to get it right," he said.

Josh concluded that for trace scheduling to be effective, he needed a different kind of computer, one designed with trace scheduling in mind. The way computers were being designed then wasn't going to work—with hardware people in charge of the architecture and when they were done "throwing it over the wall" for the software engineers to do their piece. Since trace scheduling was a software technique, the software guys needed to be part of the first team, the architecture design team, as first class collaborators with the hardware engineers.

When Josh saw a computer using trace scheduling in his mind, he saw an entirely different style of computer, one built to use automatically generated code. Operations to be done at the same time would be bunched into "instruction words;" the longer the "instruction word," the more parallelism available. And since all the hard work would be done by the trace scheduling module of the compiler as it translated the programmer's language into machine language, no hand coding would be needed and the computer itself could be an ordinary computer which could run any program, not a single purpose machine.

The new computer would be simple, with all the parts that modern computers have, including caches, adders and memory buses. Since there would be more going on, with more operations done in parallel, there would be more of each part: more caches, adders and memory buses, all working at the same time. And, because it would be designed for the compiler, there wouldn't be extraneous idiosyncratic hardware to side-track it, the way there was on the FPS machine.

This was what Josh needed in order to produce the performance speed-up trace scheduling promised, a hardware platform built especially for it: a new computer— a simple, general purpose, high performance computer, designed with trace scheduling in mind.

"It looks like we have to build our own machine," he said.

But Josh wasn't ready to design the computer yet. He needed the trace scheduling compiler to tell him what kind of architecture was best. Without it, he would be guessing which hardware was most effective for code generated by trace scheduling, which configuration. And the compiler implementing trace scheduling hadn't been written yet. This was the implementation that Jack Schwartz had wanted in Josh's PhD thesis.

Over the next two years, Josh and his graduate students John Ellis, Alex Nicolau and John Ruttenberg wrote the Bulldog Compiler. The students had signed onto Josh's project early, interested by the promise of trace scheduling. Their work on the Bulldog Compiler became the basis for their PhD theses, just as Josh's work on PUMA had become his thesis. In fact, the following year, John Ellis's thesis was selected by the ACM as the best computer science dissertation of the year.

During the summer of 1982, Josh worked at home and wrote the trace scheduler. When that and the rest of the compiler were ready, he saw what the code produced by trace scheduling would look like. Then he, with help from John Ruttenberg, began work on the architecture for a computer designed in an entirely new style, a computer designed with the compiler in mind.

* * *

It is amazing that Josh was able to be as productive as he was during his first years at Yale, the years we lived in Darien, each of us working forty miles away from home. We lived and worked this way because we both had jobs we loved, but in Darien we endured chaos and anguishing worry, with unreliable childcare, my second pregnancy, constantly sick kids, and the ordeal of trying to transport Davey to a half day of kindergarten. These problems wore us down, the next problem worse than the one before it. After four years, Josh's intense work and travel schedule combined with our three hour daily commutes wore our family to the breaking point.

By that time I had worked at the Equitable for nine years, first in legislative compliance, then in product development and then promoted into management. I had begun the job after several false starts, and at the Equitable I found strengths I didn't know I had. It became the center of my life, the source of my personal feelings of competence and I learned something new every day. But having children changed me in ways I hadn't imagined, and the problems we had in Darien went to my heart.

When our second child, Dorothy, was born in January, 1982, she had allergies and ear infections and was constantly sick. After a three month maternity leave spent largely taking Dorrie to the doctor, I handed the daytime childcare over to Josh, whose classes were over for the summer. He worked from home, writing the trace scheduler, taking Dorrie to the doctor and to Diane, Davey's longtime babysitter, for a few hours every day so that he could work more productively. Josh was comfortable with this schedule, happy that he could be available for his kids while I was 40 miles away in New York City. I was happy, too, knowing the kids were well taken care of. We began to think that our lives would regain equilibrium.

Then late that summer Diane's children got sick and Davey got sick, too, with his sickness turning into Scarlet Fever. This disease is just a strep throat with a skin rash, treatable with penicillin, no longer the killer it was in the 1800s, but even though Davey recovered quickly, it scared Josh and me pretty badly. The next month Josh returned to Yale and Davey started kindergarten—and things really got complicated. The school bus wouldn't drop Davey at Diane's after kindergarten because she lived across the town line in Stamford. There was no after school care or private children's transportation then, either, and since Josh and I each worked forty miles away, neither of us could drive Davey in the middle of our workday. We didn't want to find other childcare in Darien because Davey was attached to Diane and to her kids, too. He had had so much disruption in his life already; we were afraid that separating them would hurt him.

We decided to hire a second babysitter to stay with Dorrie in the mornings, pick Davey up at kindergarten and take both children to Diane for the afternoon. We hired someone who answered our ad, but our new morning babysitter quit after two weeks. The next person lasted a few months, then quit, and we found someone else. It was very discouraging and wearing on both of us, but we couldn't seem to find reliable people. Josh and I were getting more and more tired, but we didn't know what to do.

Josh had found an exciting new world at Yale; his research was beginning to look important. And for me, so much of my self-image was centered on my work. Neither of us wanted the other to quit. We didn't fight; we were beyond fighting—we were too exhausted. There was nothing to fight about, anyway, even though what we were doing was not working. We kept hoping that things would get better or that we would find a solution. But the chaos was wearing us down, and life was grim. We loved our jobs and our family; we had no answers. We just kept doggedly at it.

VLIW

In the fall of 1982 Josh began talking publicly about hardware, about a new style of computer, designed to run trace scheduled code. He called this style VLIW, Very Long Instruction Word technology. To officially launch it, he submitted a paper to the International Symposium of Computer Architecture, the most influential architecture forum, for a conference to be held the following June in Stockholm.

To help him with the ISCA paper, he hired Mary-Claire Van Leunen, a departmental grant writer whose recently published book, *A Handbook for Scholars,* was a bible in the Yale Computer Science Department. Famously prickly and outspoken, she held a going-away party for one of the departing faculty, a celebration—after he left. Mary-Claire was an honorary member of the Tools Group.

It took Josh a while to warm to Mary-Claire because she had many strict rules for academic papers. She thought they were mostly poorly written by the scientific community—and she was adamant. At first Josh thought her expertise was limited to "fourteen rules about commas" and reference citations, but when she told him that academic writing was like writing programs, that the goal was simplicity, transparency and clarity, he realized that she was someone who knew a lot.

"Only one idea per paragraph," said Mary-Claire. "As simple as possible."

She encouraged Josh to name his computer the ELI-512, Enormously Long Instructions, saying everyone would know that it "wasn't invented at Harvard," since Yalies were called Elis after Elihu Yale. In the computer name, 512 was the number of bits in each instruction word.

Article on the ELI-512 in the Yale Daily News, April, 1983

With Mary-Claire's help and months of work, Josh's ISCA paper was beautifully written: simple and clear. Because of her lessons, his reviews said, "This is such a clearly written paper it should be published on those grounds alone," but also, "This paper was written in an annoyingly juvenile style," which Josh took as a compliment.

* * *

While Josh swung into high gear on his hardware technology, our home life in Darien continued to be chaotic. Dorrie's allergies and ear infections continued and so did our unreliable childcare. And we were both still spending three hours of every day commuting. We were holding our world together as best we could, but we were exhausted, finding our lives a struggle.

Then on March 7, 1983, the Metro North Railroad, which we both took to work, went on strike. The strike lasted for six weeks.

Josh began driving, and I found a ride to the end of the subway line with the husband of Davey's babysitter who worked near my office in New York. My commute began taking four to six hours every day since the extra ninety thousand strike-stranded people created terrible traffic jams getting into New York City. It was horrible, wearing on Josh and me and on our kids.

After the strike had been going for four weeks, Dorrie became sick, sicker than she had ever been, with a high fever and diarrhea. We had a new babysitter then to care for Dorrie at home in the mornings, an eighteen-year-old girl we had not been thrilled about hiring but who seemed like the best of a mediocre lot of applicants.

The morning after Dorrie got sick Josh had been unhappy about leaving, but he had to teach a class. Several hours after he left, around mid-morning, he called the babysitter to find out how Dorrie was. She told Josh that Dorrie hadn't wanted to get up, that she was "just lying there," so the babysitter was letting her sleep. That was very unlike Dorrie who, at fourteen months, was a lively, happy child no matter how sick she was. Realizing that he couldn't leave his sick child with someone whose judgment he didn't trust, Josh raced home, frantically breaking speed limits on Interstate 95.

When he got home, he quickly took Dorrie to the pediatrician who prescribed medicine and Pedialyte for rehydration but who also said that if there was no improvement by that evening, we would have to bring her to the hospital. The pediatric practice had lost a child to diarrhea the previous year, so now they were very cautious.

When I got home from work, finally, having been marooned in New York until my evening ride, I was horrified to see how sick Dorrie was. She had not improved since Josh took her to the doctor, so we took her to the hospital, leaving five-year-old Davey with Diane. As we drove there I told Davey that the doctors were going to "make Dorrie all better." He looked frightened and asked "what if they can't?" and I realized how worried my five-year-old was—how worried we all were, afraid for our baby's life.

Josh and I stayed home from work during Dorrie's three days in the hospital, sleeping in a recliner in her room. She responded quickly to rehydration therapy and soon her fever was down. We took her home from the hospital and our entire family collapsed from exhaustion. We were completely spent, depleted not just from the crisis that had passed, but from the entire last hard year with the kids' sickness and all the turmoil in our childcare. Josh and I both knew that we were at the end of our ability to cope.

Over the next few days and weeks we discussed ways to work out our problems, tossing around solutions the way we had for the past few years—but now we were talking about bigger changes. Josh thought he had the answer. He said we had to move back to Teaneck where his Aunt Betty lived. He would drive to Yale or, if that didn't work, get a different job so that he could be available to his family.

If Josh had told me I had to quit my job, I wouldn't have stood for it. We would have fought and nothing constructive would have come of it. But he would never say or think anything like that. That was not the way Josh was or the way our relationship worked. His solution was to sacrifice himself, and I knew he meant what he said—but his solution didn't sound practical to me. I didn't believe Josh could drive to Yale from Teaneck; he would end up quitting his job, leaving Yale. It made me think long and hard about myself.

When I started at the Equitable nine years earlier, I thought it was the most exciting place I had ever been; it seemed as though there was no limit to what I could do or where I could go. Apart from Josh, it was the only really important thing in my life. And when the kids came, I thought I had everything—a job I loved, my wonderful husband and my kids. That was why I had stayed so long at the Equitable, put up with all the hardship of living in Darien. Josh and I were trying to do something ambitious: managing two careers in different cities and children, too, without an adequate support system. Maybe it was just too hard for us to do.

When Dorrie got sick, I realized how much my priorities had changed without my noticing. Calling my mother from the hospital to tell her about Dorrie's illness, I found that I couldn't bring my mind back to work when she asked about my job. The week before, I had been eager to talk about my career, but now I couldn't think of anything to say. I just stood there in the hospital break room with the phone in my hand.

My life at the Equitable was different now, too; the days when I learned something new every day were past. My last few job changes had been lateral, not involving promotions, and I thought I might have hit the "glass ceiling." I thought I might need an MBA to get farther up the career ladder. I realized that if either Josh or I had to give up a job, it needed to be me, no matter how painful it was. Ten years earlier it would have been different, when Josh was going from job to job, not sure of what he wanted to do. Then, his work was too unreliable to count on; now he was settled, reliable and stable, with a bright career ahead of him. Tenure at Yale was in the air. With trace scheduling, VLIW, the research group, the grants, I knew I couldn't let Josh leave Yale. I couldn't let us move back to Teaneck.

With a lot of regret, I left my job at the Equitable and we moved to the New Haven area. Our wise friend from NYU, Martin Davis, told us that the life we had led in Darien had never made sense to him; it seemed like something people did only when they had to—like in wartime. When we moved, we discovered that Martin was right; it was a relief when we stopped.

The change was hard for me, especially at first. I had been an insurance executive wearing a "power suit" and now I was a housewife wearing jeans, preparing to start an MBA program as soon as I could. But everyone in our family relaxed, un-kinking from our hard years. And the new house in Woodbridge, CT, was a refuge on three acres of woods, next to a wilderness owned by the water

Our house in Woodbridge, outside New Haven

company. After fighting so hard to maintain a life that wasn't working, we needed the peace this tranquil spot gave us.

In June, 1983, right before we moved, Josh flew to Rochester with both kids, leaving them with his parents. He then flew to Stockholm to present his paper while I finished my last days at the Equitable. I met Josh in London after he gave his paper while the Darien real estate agent's son packed our belongings. Then we flew home, moved our household from Darien to Woodbridge, and picked up our kids in Rochester. After all this, Josh was so exhausted that on the way back from the airport he fell asleep while driving. He recovered quickly, not going off the road, but he was shocked to find out, so dangerously, how exhausted he was.

* * *

The Stockholm conference, ISCA, was Josh's first international conference, his first time in Europe, and he was eager for new experiences. When he called me at home from the conference, I remembered my own trip to Europe almost twenty years before, how thrilling it had been. People just like me living entirely differently, in ways I never imagined. I remembered that pleasure and after our hard years in Darien, I was glad Josh was experiencing it now.

The conference was held at the center where the Nobel prizes are awarded; the "outing" was an official tour of the palace. Since it was June, the light got dim at 11pm, but the midnight sun never really went down. Between sessions and after hours, Josh walked the streets of Stockholm, stopping in coffee houses, seeing as much of the city as he could, talking to all the friendly blond people. Josh found Stockholm to be an amazing place.

Decades later, Josh's paper introducing VLIW technology was voted one of the most influential in ISCA history but, in 1983, it wasn't received that way. Josh had prepared carefully, with Mary-Claire's help, and he had looked forward to sharing his research. But instead of the positive reaction he expected, no one at ISCA thought VLIW was practical. They didn't laugh or ridicule him when he presented his paper, but the very description of the software-driven technology seemed impossible to them. They thought Josh's ideas were a little crazy but interesting in an academic way, as something that might someday add to the field of knowledge but not anything that could ever be built. There wasn't even the eager clamor of questions he was used to.

Josh was confused and terribly disappointed by this reception. He had no idea this could happen; he was not prepared for colleagues unwilling to listen to his research results. He knew the ideas he was presenting were new, but he had expected objectivity. Since scientists change their beliefs when evidence points in a different direction, he thought that if he explained his work well enough, its truth would be evident.

He left Stockholm knowing that he had a lot of work ahead of him, that he would have to fight to get his research accepted. We were moving to Woodbridge for an easier life for our family, but now it looked as though Josh needed to use the time he was gaining to fight for his academic life.

When Josh got back to Yale, the first thing he had to do was figure out what was going on. His architecture colleagues across the country had loved trace scheduling, his software technique. They knew it could make machines faster; it was very successful. VLIW was simply technology built to use it effectively—that was all. Why wouldn't they also like VLIW technology? Why couldn't they see its use in general computers? Or understand that software engineers needed to have a significant part in designing the architecture?

Colleagues he thought were sensible were saying things that made no sense. They were saying that a VLIW computer was "impossible to build." Impossible to build? How could that be? The hardware was the easiest part of a VLIW; it was far simpler than that used by the current general purpose computers which found parallelism in the hardware. It was the software, the compiler, that was tricky and everyone knew that trace scheduling software worked. No one was arguing about that.

Little by little the problem became clear. And the answer solved a mystery that had been confusing Josh since he started talking about hardware: his audiences were small for trace scheduling, but when he started talking about hardware, he could fill any room. So many people showing up to tell him he was wrong—so much frenzy and noise.

"You can get a lot more people, a *lot* more people, to come to your talk if you promise them bizarre-sounding hardware instead of a compiler technique," he said.

Why this sudden change? Why when he switched from talking about software to talking about hardware was there suddenly all this opposition? Why did the enthusiastic, subdued trace scheduling audiences turn into frenetically opposed VLIW audiences? Why was there an electric energy, an excitement, about VLIW technology that was missing when he talked about trace scheduling?

As Josh puzzled through it, he realized that while the industry put compilers on a pedestal, it was something they gave lip service to but didn't follow through on. Computer companies thought they wanted strong compiler engineers involved but they didn't work that way. They couldn't imagine a compiler writer with veto power over any part of the hardware.

It turns out that when Josh entered hardware research, he touched an area with far more glamour and more entrenched interests than anything he had ever been near. Hardware designers were the flashy figures in the industry—the cowboys, the test pilots—used to being in full charge of design and they had always controlled computer architecture. Now Josh was proposing that different people, software engineers, be put in charge of important parts of the architecture, making a grab for the most fundamental part of the process. When he suggested that software engineers would be full partners with the hardware guys, he was suggesting something unimaginable.

When Glen Culler stood up after a talk and told the audience, very emotionally, how much Culler Scientific could have used him when they designed the Floating Point Systems machine, Josh looked at him silently, knowing how unlikely it was that he would have been put in charge of the architecture. He realized that Glen had no idea that was what he was suggesting, no idea that for Josh's technology to be effective at Culler, the compiler guys would have had to lead the architecture design.

At that point in his life, Josh knew nothing about the academic and industry pecking order; he blundered into a power structure he never knew existed. He had been educated at NYU, the home of compiler expertise, outside the mainstream of general computer science. He didn't know that engineers who did software were afterthoughts in the industry. He had no idea how extreme his proposal was, no idea how radical the idea of a compiler-driven computer architecture was when he first suggested it.

It seems pretty audacious for a young faculty member to propose the kind of revolution that Josh was putting forward. At first he didn't realize how far-reaching his ideas were, thinking he was only putting forth a hardware platform for trace scheduling, simply a new computer among many. But pretty quickly, he came to believe that VLIW technology went far beyond an academic project, that it had the potential to change all of scientific computing.

Overnight Josh went from being a bright junior faculty member with an interesting software technique to someone who wanted to take over the most glamorous part of computers, from working for the hardware experts to wanting the hardware experts to work for him. His persuasive abilities, his salesmanship, only made it worse. He published papers with inflammatory, self-righteous titles like *VLIW Machines: Multiprocessors We Can Actually Program* and *Parallel Processing: A Smart Compiler and a Dumb Machine*, written in the clear, Mary-Claire style so that everyone could understand them. He faced furious opposition.

Life was not pretty. Josh was visible in the computer science community, the way Roger, the Yale Chair, wanted him to be, on his way to being a star, but he didn't like it. He wanted acceptance for his work, not notoriety. Every night he came home for dinner more confused and more upset, telling me about his setbacks. And I could see them clearly now that I had more time and energy to pay attention—and I was worried. Josh was constantly on the phone or on the computer, trying to convince people, trying to find a way to express his ideas so that their truth would be evident to everyone.

The idea of the hardware and the programs that run on them looking alike was not completely new. The FPS machine worked that way. But in 1983 these technologies had limited use because they had to be hand programmed and that was very time consuming. Josh was not talking about building one of these specialized niche market computers; he was talking about a computer which could automatically run any program. And he was saying that VLIW machines, his technology, could produce much higher performance at much lower cost than any of the current general-purpose computers.

Much higher performance. At much lower cost. On any program. This was revolutionary. Josh was going against the big boys.

He was a "young man in a hurry," not content to accept his colleagues' assessment of his technology, not content to merely add to the field of knowledge. He was convinced it was practical and didn't want to wait for the academic world to catch up. He wanted his computer built, as an actual machine, and he wanted it built now.

* * *

In the middle of all this, Josh and his group continued working on Bulldog, the trace scheduling compiler, so that they could figure out which architecture a VLIW computer should run. Some of the Tools Group worked on the project and there was a synergy, the Tools Group members not on the project spurring everyone to better results, all of them using the principles Alan Perlis had taught them. And Josh was in there with the rest, providing technical leadership but writing code, too, the whole group working at desks littered with empty soda cans.

Josh had to fight the funding agencies to put terminals and modems in the students' homes. No one did that back then; people thought it was a fanciful extravagance, as though you were providing them with luxury cars. But he didn't care when, where or how his students worked: he just cared about results—unusual in the days before widespread telecommuting.

"They will work until bedtime!" Josh told the funding agencies. "You get much more work out of them this way, and for free."

Finally, the NSF program officer said, "Just lie,"— meaning that Josh should hide the money in his grant proposal.

"Okay," said Josh and, after that, the students worked from home.

And the results they were getting were dramatic: John Ellis' thesis defense startled the Yale faculty with evidence that the technology could produce dramatic speedup, sometimes ten to thirty times, on the simulator running code generated by the Bulldog Compiler. No one thought the speedup would be that dramatic on a real machine, but it looked as though it would be the most effective computer at anywhere near the price, cycling faster and requiring less hardware.

As Josh's research group worked, he continued traveling, trying to get his colleagues to accept his research. He kept drawing large audiences, but the objections went on and on. People he respected were standing up, saying that what Josh proposed wouldn't work or couldn't be built, as though he were proposing some sort of Frankenstein monster.

When he asked "why not," why couldn't a VLIW computer be built, he found the answers inarticulate. Finally, he decided that the only sense he could make of it was that no one had ever done this before; that his colleagues seemed to be saying that if it worked, someone else would have thought it up by now. This seemed like know-nothing-ism to Josh, and he was disgusted.

Science was not enough for the computer science community. All his talking, all his research and data, were getting him nowhere. He needed to stop trying to convince the academic world, and turn to the computer industry. In pursuit of profit, Josh thought that industry would be more interested in an effective technology than his academic colleagues who were stuck in their own theories.

But would this work? Would the scientific computing industry pay attention to him? How could Josh have been arrogant enough to believe that he could propose a technology that would fundamentally change the industry? In 1983, this idea was not as implausible as it seems.

Thirty years ago computers in general use were new, and innovative technologies were popping up everywhere. Companies that didn't exist the month before were producing odd machines with exotic hardware, starting up and going out of business every day. You could produce a computer in your garage, have your technology catch on and make a fortune—anything could happen. Why not a computer based on software innovation instead of exotic hardware? Why not a new technology, coming out of Yale, revolutionizing the industry?

JOHN AND JOHN

At Yale, Josh organized his group to build a working model of the computer described in his ISCA paper. John O'Donnell and some of the students worked on the project, and Josh hired a hardware engineer John knew to begin the implementation. When it was ready, he planned to approach industry to get it out into the marketplace where it could prove its worth.

Quickly, though, the job proved far too big, hopelessly beyond the scope of an academic project. A real machine was a vast undertaking and took lots of money. It needed more full-time hardware designers than Josh could afford; his grants were for funding students and departmental computers, not manufacturing.

Josh found the project hopeless and started to ignore it, irritating John O'Donnell. Josh and the students knew the job was too big, but John never thought anything was beyond him.

John was an unusual person, tall and thin with a high forehead and boundless energy and optimism but harboring an internal war between the practical and the academic that he never fully resolved. He had such extreme intelligence and manic energy that there seemed no limit to his abilities. He had a genius for putting things together with creativity and accuracy, working productively night and day, driving the people around him to work harder than anyone thought possible. People said that if you wanted a cardboard box factory, for instance, you could send him to study one and a week later you would have it, even though he knew nothing about cardboard box factories a week earlier.

Ideally, he wanted to do science but he could never sit still long enough. His mind was too active and, since he could do anything, he tried to do everything, to build everything in sight, a hundred things at a hundred miles per hour. And he was so smart that it seemed like he could do it all.

John O'Donnell in his office

In 1980, when Roger Shank became Department Chair, he wanted a creative Facilities Manager, one who could bring the department into the new era of workstations and minicomputers. He knew John from his days as a Yale undergraduate, but John had gone off to Princeton as a graduate student to study astrophysics. Roger heard that at Princeton, though still intending to study, John was spending most of his time setting up and managing the computers for the Astrophysics Department. Roger offered him the Facilities Manager job at Yale and to tempt John away from Princeton, Roger gave him his choice of outlets to satisfy his interests and energy; he could become involved in any departmental project and also get a PhD, if he wanted.

Soon after he arrived at Yale, John became interested in trace scheduling, plunging into the project. Eventually, he got a research appointment, enabling him to teach classes, and in 1984 he and Josh taught the computer architecture class together. His strange status didn't bother Josh who had taught graduate classes as an undergraduate at NYU. He looked at John, saw his ability and put him to work.

It took John a while to accept that the job of designing and building a working model of the VLIW computer was too big for Josh's group, but when he did, he suggested that he and Josh contact the large computer companies to see if any of them were interested. He imagined a joint research and development project, the company completing the prototype design and building the machine with advice and help from the Yale group. This would be a major commitment for the computer company, but John was convinced that there would be a big payoff in industry domination and profit for whoever took it on.

Josh liked this idea; John's suggestion came at a good time. After the skepticism in Stockholm, Josh was anxious to prove the worth of the technology to his colleagues. This seemed like something that would work.

Josh and John approached Digital Equipment, IBM, Texas Instruments, and Honeywell, among others. All the companies were interested and sent teams to Yale to evaluate the technology. Josh's group did presentations, highlighting the research and the results—how fast a VLIW computer could go.

Meetings followed meetings. There was lots of interest, a lot of activity, but little follow-through from the companies, frustrating everyone involved in putting together the dog-and-pony shows. No offers were coming back.

Josh had little business experience and no understanding of large companies, so when IBM sent its third evaluation team—which didn't know about the other IBM teams—he angrily threw them out of his office, thinking it a waste of everyone's time. That didn't stop the interest, though, and the visits continued through the summer and fall of 1983. And the Yale group kept doing presentations.

* * *

John Ruttenberg had been following this unsuccessful progress, the parade of technology companies visiting the group. He was Josh's first graduate student, having wandered into Josh's office early in the fall of 1979. He liked Josh's research and wanted to write his PhD with him. Startled, Josh was so new then that he had to figure out what he needed to do to officially have a graduate student. Ruttenberg helped him through the administration and had been on the project ever since, growing as the project grew.

John was raised with extreme wealth, the oldest son of industrialist Derald Ruttenberg, who is credited with inventing leveraged buy-outs in the 1950s. He grew up in his family's homes on Sutton Place in New York City, in Bucks County, PA and in the Dominican Republic. There was also an estate in Scotland when Josh met him, but that was a later addition, not part of John's upbringing. A few years after Josh met him, John's father gave first $7 million and then an additional $8 million to Mt. Sinai

Hospital in New York City. Financial arrangements with John, beyond spending money, were always very complicated, involving checks from different trust accounts. He was the only Yale CS graduate student paying his own tuition, not supported by grants, something that made people think he was a dilettante until they got to know his work.

In the fall of 1983, John sat down with Josh and John O'Donnell. He had been watching the computer companies reviewing the project and he had some thoughts.

"This isn't how big companies work," he said. "IBM or Honeywell can be truly interested, but a company that size is too conservative to invest in something as untested as VLIW."

Ruttenberg suggested that instead of continuing to court a computer giant, they form their own company to develop VLIW computers, financed by venture capital.

John Ruttenberg explains

"Start-ups aren't my family's business, but we have lots of contacts in the venture community," John said. "There will be plenty of investors to finance us. I'll be a founder, along with the two of you. We can do this—and we'll all get rich."

John Ruttenberg had an intuitive understanding of business, absorbed at the family dinner table, a deep knowledge of how that world worked and the financial underpinnings of success. He understood the mechanics of wealth creation, using that phrase a lot. And he knew about companies at all stages of their lives: new, mature, dying and being restructured. For him, starting a company to commercialize new technology was a natural step. It didn't seem strange at all. And he was convinced it was possible.

* * *

During the early and mid 1980s, there was a venture-financed boom in small computer companies that rivaled the dot-com boom of the 1990s and, in the fall of 1983, that boom was at its height. The thinking was, "if it wiggled, fund it." So many academic computer scientists were leaving universities to start companies that the National Science Foundation began a program, the Presidential Young Investigator Award, a $250,000 grant for computer scientists under age forty willing to stay at universities. Josh had been honored to win one of these awards in 1982, the first year they were given, when there was a backlog of deserving candidates.

Applying for the PYI grant, Josh's commitment to stay at Yale was real. When he envisioned a company building a VLIW computer he, like John O'Donnell, pictured a partnership with his group at Yale providing guidance to industrial manufacturers. He never pictured *being* the industrial manufacturer. He loved being a professor and couldn't imagine his life anywhere else. He was a researcher, not a businessman.

But as soon as Ruttenberg suggested a start-up, O'Donnell wanted to do it. His family had been involved with the founding of Hertz Rental Car; he thought the idea of a venture funded company was great—and natural. They could control all aspects of the design, get good people— the people in the Yale group—and charge ahead. He wanted to get right to it; it was a perfect outlet for his energy.

Both of them, O'Donnell and Ruttenberg, were confident that the three of them could make it work. O'Donnell would run hardware and Ruttenberg would run the compiler group, all under Josh's leadership. They had been working with the technology for so long that they had developed a deep understanding of it—as had the whole Yale group. If the computer was going to be built, these were the people to do it.

Of the three of them, only Josh had trouble with the idea. He couldn't get his mind around an entrepreneurial company founded to produce computers using his technology. He couldn't imagine their doing it or his working there. But Josh wanted to see the technology built and no big company had shown any sign of taking up the challenge. He cared about his group, the students who had put so much of themselves into the work; he wanted it to go somewhere. And he couldn't imagine a computer start-up based on his technology happening without him.

Could he do both jobs—Yale and a start-up? He had colleagues who did it, running companies based on their research, managing to combine that with an active academic career. These businesses were small, though, mainly consulting or software companies with just a few employees, not all-consuming commitments like

Ruttenberg was suggesting. They provided a good income, but Josh had reservations about mixing research with a profit-making venture, particularly one that employed his students. It seemed as though there was a built-in conflict of interest. He was also worried about adequately accounting for time and resources when juggling his grants, especially when his personal income depended on his decisions.

And Ruttenberg was not proposing anything small. He envisioned a company designing and building computers, maybe even marketing them. Josh knew people at companies like that, venture-funded businesses like Ruttenberg was suggesting: Apollo, Floating Point Systems, Mentor Graphics and Sun. People at these companies were consumed; their every waking moment was spent involved with the business. They had no time for anything but their work, not even their families, and many of them got divorced. Josh simply could not imagine himself at a company like that.

Because both John and John liked the idea of a start-up, though, Josh let Ruttenberg make some calls, despite how unlikely the whole thing seemed. John invited VCs at Fairfield Venture Partners, a Stamford, CT firm, to spend an afternoon at Yale in September, 1983, meeting with Josh and his group to explain what venture funding was all about.

Pedro Castillo, a Cuban émigré and old friend of the Ruttenberg family, brought Gene Petinelli, a junior partner, as well as several others. They gave the Yalies a shopping list of everything they needed if they wanted to go forward—a realistic business plan leading to profitability and the personnel to make it happen. If the deal was approved, the VCs would fund the company in partnership with other venture firms, getting majority ownership in the new company in exchange for their backing. The VCs also said that a company intending to build and market computers needed an experienced leader as CEO, but not one of them since they had no business experience.

The meeting made very little impression on Josh; he was really just indulging Ruttenberg. A venture-funded start-up still seemed outlandish; his mind was not fully around the idea. But Josh stayed through the meeting, knowing that his group wanted to go forward, and that this was a way to do it. And as time went on, the idea of a start-up became more concrete even to Josh. During the fall there were other discussions with Fairfield Ventures, and Josh began to think about it—seriously.

* * *

For my part, I was horrified by the thought of Josh's leaving Yale for a computer start-up and couldn't understand why he was considering it—just when he was on the verge of becoming an academic star. Only a few months earlier I had left a secure job which provided health insurance for our whole family; Josh earned our family's only income now and I was terrified of losing it. After the hard life we had in Darien, we were supposed to be recovering now, relaxing in a less stressful life. What could be more stressful than starting a business? It seemed crazy to me—incredibly grueling and risky. Two years earlier Josh had been promoted to Associate Professor; he expected tenure in 1984. Yale was everything he had ever wanted and everything I had ever wanted for him. I was beside myself; I couldn't understand giving all of this up.

Also, it was hard for me to get my mind around the idea that my husband of almost twenty years, whom I had married when we were both students, had invented technology that could change the world. I understood Josh's career at Yale, and that looked wonderful to me—with his students, all the grant funding, and his technology research. But now he was talking about people investing millions of dollars in a business that could become the next DEC. It wasn't that I didn't believe in him; I just found the scale so big that it was outside my comprehension.

When I talked to my father, though, voicing my doubts, he said that I shouldn't be so sure that Josh's leaving Yale for a start-up was the wrong move. He had been impressed with Josh's ability to "land on his feet" through all our hard years and thought that big things might result. It was true; Josh was very resourceful and, certainly, I did want Josh's scientific vision to be vindicated. And Ruttenberg was right that no large computer manufacturer was interested enough to build the VLIW computer with the Yale group.

John and John talked about the potential for great wealth, and I knew that a lot of start-up founders got rich when the companies went public. I liked that idea, but I had trouble believing in it, since so many more companies failed than succeeded. A computer start-up seemed particularly risky to me, since it had to be so big. It reminded me of a lottery ticket, where someone does actually win millions of dollars, but the chances are so slim it isn't worth thinking about. You wouldn't bet your life or your career on a lottery ticket.

In February, 1984, five months after Josh began thinking about a start-up, I went to San Francisco with him when he presented a paper at a conference. On that trip we spent hours walking up and down the San Francisco hills, talking about Josh's future, debating the pros and cons of all the alternatives, talking through what it would mean for our lives. I had been so involved with my own work and with our kids' troubles that I hadn't paid close enough attention to specifics. Now, away from the kids and our day-to-day issues, I told Josh about my fears—but also about my hopes for him. And he poured out all his thoughts and feelings, his strong belief in his technology and his ambitions for it, and his thoughts about a start-up.

In the months since Ruttenberg first proposed starting a company, Josh's thinking had evolved quite a bit. At Yale, Josh hated all the time he needed to spend chasing grant money, hated how political and prone to following the latest fashions most of the funding agencies were. He came to think that a new company would free up his time for building and working with his group, that he wouldn't have to spend so much time raising money. Also, he had faith in the free market. He thought that profitability would be the only issue he had to fight, envisioning a purity free of colleagues defending turf with wrong-headed theories. This didn't sound like the business world I had worked in, but Josh believed in it. He was convinced that here was the place for VLIW technology to prove its worth. And he wanted to try it.

As we walked, I listened to what Josh was saying and thought back to my talks with John and John. They looked at a start-up as the logical outgrowth of the VLIW research and their partnership was important to them. As we talked, walking in San Francisco, Josh's excitement started grabbing me, the momentum that was pulling all the guys. I saw VLIW as something real, not just an academic project. And for the first time I began to see the company they were talking about; it didn't seem so impossible. I realized that I couldn't stand in the way of whatever was next for Josh and VLIW. If leaving Yale was the only way he could get his machine built, then our family would adapt in whatever way we needed. We would trust fate and hope for the best. Maybe they would change the world.

After our talk, Josh decided to continue exploring options for a start-up, seeing where it took him—now with my blessing. He left the question of his role in a new company alone, thinking that it would answer itself. He was not a businessman, but he was the leader of his group, and he knew he needed to be fully involved or his group would not commit 100%. He did not expect to leave Yale, but thought he might take a leave of absence, returning as soon as the company got on its feet.

When word leaked to the Computer Science Department that Josh and his group were thinking of leaving to do a start-up, there was an uproar. Colleague after colleague asked him to stay. When Martin and Beverly Schultz had dinner at our house during this time, even Beverly—the faculty wife—tried to talk him out of leaving. But Josh wanted to build his computer.

THREE GUYS AND A CAR

Before Josh, Ruttenberg, and O'Donnell got too far along with the venture capitalists, something new popped up and they found themselves going in a different direction.

Apollo Computer was a workstation company O'Donnell brought to Yale to supply departmental computers. It was founded in 1980 and had recently gone public, making the founders millionaires many times over. Josh and O'Donnell hadn't approached Apollo the summer before to build the VLIW machine because they thought it was too small with too many growing pains to dedicate a team to a new technology, even with the advice of the Yale group. But O'Donnell had been encouraging the founders to invest in the company he was starting.

Apollo wanted to get into the market for higher performance computers and saw a lot of potential in Josh's technology. In October, 1983, Josh, John and John drove to Apollo headquarters in Chelmsford, MA to meet with Mike Greata, a founder and vice president of engineering in charge of new ventures, to see if there was any business they could do together. They met all day, Greata looking at the business plan they had put together for the VCs. He liked what he saw and had an innovative idea.

Greata suggested that instead of investing, Apollo might want to entirely fund the new company, cutting out the venture capitalists completely. The new company would design the computer and Apollo would manufacture and market it as its own product. Eventually, Apollo would buy them out. This would be good for both groups, Greata told them. The Yale group would have funds to develop the computer and Apollo would have a new product, giving them entrée into the high performance market.

This was a startling development—something new to think about. They told Mike they would consider it seriously and went home to get their minds around the new idea.

The three of them had focused on VC financing since the meeting with Fairfield Ventures the month before, but this seemed even better—much less risky. With funding from Apollo, the new company could do what Josh's group had always been good at—designing and building technology—and leave manufacturing, marketing and sales to people who knew how to do them. They might not get as rich, but there was a much smaller down-side risk, since funding would be assured. Even Ruttenberg, such a proponent of venture capitalism, thought a deal with Apollo was preferable to going it alone.

By November 9, 1983, when Josh, Ruttenberg and O'Donnell drove to the Apollo headquarters for the next serious meetings, they had become convinced that a deal with Apollo was probably the best way to build the computer. In the months since Ruttenberg first proposed starting a company, Josh and the Johns had done a lot of work. They had talked to people throughout the industry, written business plans, generally geared themselves up so that they knew more about what a start-up would entail. And they started interviewing CEO candidates, calling everyone the VCs recommended.

Over the Thanksgiving break in 1983, while we were visiting my brother and his family, now living in Burlington, VT, Josh flew into Boston to interview a CEO candidate in a meeting room at Logan airport. He flew accident-prone Provincetown-Boston Airlines in a five passenger Piper Aztec puddle jumper, taking off in a blinding snowstorm. The scene was bizarre:

"Hey, Bob; you got any more barf bags? I used mine up on the last flight," the pilot called, rolling down his window as the plane approached the Burlington runway to take off for Boston.

That harrowing trip was unsuccessful—Dave Caplin, who would have made a great CEO, had no interest in moving to New Haven. No CEO candidate they talked to wanted to join them, and Josh's Boston trip convinced them they were unlikely to recruit anyone. But a company they started with Apollo backing would be much smaller than a venture funded one. They wouldn't need a high powered CEO and, since they couldn't find one, they could see how many fewer obstacles there would be to an Apollo-funded company.

On Tuesday, November 29, four days after Josh's Boston trip, they drove back to Chelmsford for a full day of meetings with Greata to begin hammering out the deal. The first talks were preliminary, both groups talking tentatively about how they would go ahead, what the deal would look like. It was a new world for the VLIW trio, and they were feeling their way.

For the next few months, all winter and into the spring, they met with Apollo, driving up and down Interstate 84 and the Massachusetts Turnpike to Chelmsford, three guys and a car. They drove, week after week, stopping at fast-food restaurants, a new experience for Ruttenberg, who looked dubiously at the menus. They took turns driving, and often they would be three guys and O'Donnell's diesel VW Rabbit. Once, O'Donnell tried to evade a state trooper, with Ruttenberg and Josh goading him on. After zipping by the trooper, John turned off the highway, hiding behind some hills. The trooper found them and angrily approached the car with a hand on his gun and his holster unsnapped.

"You guys are fucking with me; I don't like being fucked with," he said, ordering John and John to put their hands on the dashboard and Josh's on the seat in front of him. The guys were scared; Josh was shivering, and they apologized. It ended uneventfully, but by then they had been on the road a long time.

By spring, though, all the hard work paid off: they had a term sheet, signed by everyone, outlining the deal in principle. It would fund the new company to make a VLIW product for Apollo to market. The three guys went back to Yale and prepared to put the company together.

* * *

The Apollo meetings were always led by Mike Greata but often included the other founders. Bill Poduska was the CEO. He was an Apollo founder and had been a founder, also, of Prime Computer.

"Who's going to run this thing?" asked Poduska during one meeting.

"I will," Josh said, stepping forward.

He had been conflicted when Ruttenberg first suggested starting a company months before, but now his conflicts fell away. He had changed during the months the three of them had been on the road and he realized that without him in a leadership role, nothing would happen.

"Well, okay," said Poduska, "but you're really going to have to do it. And you're going to have to clean up your image."

He told Josh that he would have to leave Yale. And he didn't like Josh's long, straggly hair and beard or his clothes.

Leaving Yale was a hard question, one Josh did not like thinking about. He realized that for a while, at least, he would have to devote full time to the young company. What would happen after that he left alone, thinking that time would answer that question. Clothes and his personal appearance, however, were something he had to deal with right then.

Josh had always believed that no one had any business judging him by his clothes, believing in a world where character was all that counted. When he and I went to parties, he resisted dressing up, thinking my suggesting it meant that I didn't accept him for who he was. And despite his parents in the clothing business, he had had a hard time understanding that I had to buy a professional wardrobe for my job at the Equitable in New York, especially since it was so expensive.

Both Ruttenberg's and O'Donnell's families were filled with businessmen; they understood that appearances mattered and put on the right clothes without giving it a thought. But Josh dressed in the jeans and flannel shirts of a graduate student, starkly contrasting with the conservative suits and ties John and John wore when they visited Apollo or the VCs. The Johns talked to Josh about clothes early on but he resisted, adamant that it shouldn't make any difference. After a while, John and John had grim expressions on their faces, a kind of stoicism, whenever they set out for Chelmsford, and Josh could see how much his appearance bothered them.

When Poduska told Josh to clean up his image, it pushed him over a line and he realized he had to take action. He looked at John and John and saw how much clothes mattered to them—and how they felt mattered to Josh. If he was going to lead, he needed to be the leader the others wanted him to be.

I stayed out of the discussions as Josh agonized through the question of how he should dress. I had never understood what he found so hard about putting on different clothes in different circumstances.

"Just put on a tie when you need to," I thought. "It's not like you're selling your soul to the devil."

But over the years, anything I had said on the subject had ended with arguments. So, now when external pressures were pushing Josh to change his image, I stood aside and watched it happen.

Once he got his mind around his need to project a different image, Josh really did know what he should buy because of his years in his father's store. He went to Sym's and got the most conservative business suits he could find—blue pin-stripes, gray pin-stripes and a muted gray-blue plaid. He also bought white business shirts and some expensive ties and belts, shoes, and socks. Ruttenberg bought Josh his most expensive tie and then corrected the way he knotted it, changing it to something more aristocratic.

"A half Windsor knot is the way a salesman ties a tie," John said. "A gentleman uses a full Windsor knot."

John also wanted Josh to shave his beard off, saying that none of the Fortune 500 CEOs had beards, but Josh couldn't bear the thought of shaving every day. And with his new clothes, Josh now looked like a CEO despite the beard.

* * *

Josh, John and John recruited the entire Yale team and the Tools Group members who hadn't worked for Josh, too, asking them all to join the start-up. They wanted everyone, those who were working on the project and those who had finished and moved on. They went after Steve Wood at Microsoft, Bob Nix at Xerox PARC, and Geoff Lowney at NYU, former Tools Group members who hadn't worked on Josh's project and Tom Karzes at DEC who had been an undergraduate. They recruited Josh's secretary at Yale, in her mid-fifties an unlikely candidate to risk working at a computer start-up. But she really liked Josh and his group and, to everyone's pleasure, wanted to join. Alan Perlis became a real booster. When students or graduates came to him for advice, he told all of them that "Josh Fisher's project" was the most exciting place he could think of for them to work.

And I signed on too—with the company real and financed, I caught the start-up enthusiasm and wanted to be part of it. I was hired to find office space, set up employee benefits and prepare recruiting and relocation packages. The work was preliminary, since the company had no money, but they wanted to be ready to start as soon as it was available. It was fun to be working again, a lot more fun than the calculus class I was taking at Yale to prepare for my MBA or my life with the kids, driving a car pool. I was willing to wait for payment like everyone else— in the way of all start-ups—making me the ideal candidate for the job.

Apollo was putting a lot of pressure on Josh, John and John to move to Boston, calling New Haven "Silicon Nowhere." They and the venture capitalists before them thought it was a better place to attract employees, and the VCs had thought it was a better place to attract financing. But the three founders were happily settled in New Haven and didn't want to move, although O'Donnell could have been persuaded. They believed that they wouldn't have any trouble recruiting good technical people with New Haven's low cost of living; many of the technical people they wanted already lived there or had lived there before. "Silicon Nowhere" or not, New Haven was where I was looking for space.

John O'Donnell was adamant that the company office be located north of the bridge over the Quinnapiac River, the only real traffic bottleneck in the New Haven area; he and Ruttenberg both lived north. We lived south of the Q bridge, so it wasn't an issue; Josh only cared about finding the right office space. He leaned toward an urban tech start-up, but no one started tech companies in the centers of cities back then. And O'Donnell was unshakable in wanting a conventional office space, one that the engineers they recruited could recognize.

Yale was converting part of the Winchester Arms factory space into a high tech business incubator called Science Park. I liked that space, thinking the life-sized statue of John Wayne in the lobby gave it a sense of history. But in addition to its being south of the Q Bridge, the guys were worried about problems with misfiring rifles from the remaining Winchester operations. This wasn't an idle worry since the test room was right next door to the space we were considering.

We also looked at a coffin factory, which turned out to be too small, and at space owned by a college friend of Ruttenberg. During a second meeting in April, she turned to Josh.

"Oh, I see; you're the (ho, ho) CEO," she said, not believing in a company so seemingly without substance.

She broke off discussions; Josh said that, to her, they were just "three guys and a car"—and who could blame her?

But then we looked at an abandoned telephone company garage, and everyone liked it. We liked the potential landlord, too, who would build to suit, and the space was in the right area, Branford, north of the Q Bridge. When they talked about building out the space, there was discussion of whether the company really needed separate rest rooms for men and women. This terrified Josh's secretary, and he had to reassure her that the talk wasn't serious, just wild-eyed graduate student ideas. She wouldn't really have to use the rest room with the men.

* * *

In early spring of 1984, the venture capitalists started circling again. Their interest was piqued because the company had another suitor, Apollo, with a proven technology record, which took VLIW seriously. They insisted that Apollo couldn't possibly give them as good a deal as the VCs, that as naïve scientists, the founders were in no position to know what a good deal looked like.

The VCs wanted to see the term sheet describing the deal, insisting that it must be all nonsense. Josh told them not to be silly. He was inexperienced in business, but he knew *that* was wrong. They were Apollo's competition; he wasn't going to show them what Apollo was offering.

The VCs were so sure that the Apollo deal was a bad one that they offered to send the three founders to George Thibeault, a lawyer they often worked with. He was the VCs' lawyer, but he also represented established and emerging companies. If the founders consulted him now at the VCs' behest, they would be the client, assured of confidentiality, even though the VCs were paying. They said he could be impartial; George would tell them whether Apollo was taking advantage of their naïveté.

This seemed like a good idea, so on March 21, 1984, Josh met George Thibeault for dinner and showed him the term sheet. They met at the Wayside Inn in Sudbury, MA, an historic site outside of Boston, the subject of a Longfellow poem, a good place for a leisurely dinner. They talked a long time that evening, discussing mutual acquaintances and industry trends as well as Josh's technology, who was involved and, of course, the Apollo deal.

The term sheet said that Apollo would finance the start-up as a research and development company, developing the technology into a buildable design. Apollo would build and market the computer and then, after a set number of years, buy the start-up in a stock swap, the amount of stock determined by a complicated formula depending on technical milestones and on how many computers were sold.

"Everything seems to be in order," said George, " and the term sheet does have Poduska's signature on it." He told them that he liked the Apollo deal and, if they really could get it, they should do it. It looked great to him.

George was a lawyer for venture capitalists and entrepreneurs but his main interest was representing start-ups, charging below-market rates. This had paid off for him when they became large, DEC and Symbolics among them. Realizing that George saw the industry the way he did, Josh asked him to represent them in the negotiations with Apollo, waiting to be paid like everyone else—subject to the other founders' approval—and George agreed.

Why did Josh sign George up so quickly without interviewing any other lawyers? George was a special person, and it was easy for anyone to see. Short and stocky, he had a pronounced Boston accent and an unassailable aura of integrity; he radiated decency and straightforwardness. His judgment and business knowledge came through, too. He had the same perspective on the industry, believing in the same things as Josh, John and John. And he had a track record with companies they knew very well. They never regretted signing him up so quickly.

With George blessing the Apollo deal, the company founders had no more misgivings. Even the VCs were quiet now, realizing that there was a better deal here than they had thought. Everything lined up.

* * *

Apollo wanted to give the new company an initial $500,000 loan to get them going, even before finishing formal negotiations. George told them that this was fine but that anyone who signed a loan agreement would be liable for it; they needed a corporation to take the responsibility. And before they incorporated, they needed to divide up the ownership rights—the stock—and they needed to decide on a company name.

These were issues that the three founders had known about and avoided, but George spurred them to action. They had been so involved in getting funding and the mechanics of getting the company started that they had postponed all the contentious issues, putting them off as long as they could. Now they had to decide.

Dividing the company stock started out well enough. They agreed that future employees should get 50% of the stock and the founders 50%. They also agreed that Josh should get 40% of the founders' stock since without him there would be no company. Then Josh suggested that the remaining 60% of the founders' stock be divided equally between John and John. And there the agreement stopped.

Equal division was fine with Ruttenberg, but O'Donnell wouldn't hear any of it; he was adamant that he should get more stock. He said that it was obvious to everyone that he was a far more productive person than Ruttenberg, able to do six times as much and that he deserved more. Ruttenberg was equally adamant that he and O'Donnell should be treated equally, and neither would budge. For days they worked on it, Josh trying to reason with both of them. Neither would move; it was a matter of pride.

Ruttenberg had provided entrée to the money markets and the original idea for the company. And he was a gifted engineer, a compiler expert who had been one of the original authors of the Bulldog Compiler at Yale and had already accomplished so much with the technology. Also, John had a free-ranging creativity that made them consider ideas they would never have thought of, and he was even less bound by conventional thought than Josh or O'Donnell. He could say uncomfortable things no one wanted to hear, making them both face unpleasant realities, a necessary counter to O'Donnell's ambitious flights of fancy.

The company badly needed Ruttenberg, badly needed both of them. But most things Ruttenberg could do, O'Donnell had already done. O'Donnell had run big operations, was charming with investors as well as employees, a fabulous speaker and expositor. And Ruttenberg wasn't the inspiring speaker that either O'Donnell or Josh was. They reached an impasse and for days it seemed hopeless, that the new company would never be born.

Finally, Josh had an idea that Derald Ruttenberg, the great industrialist, said was inspired and showed real leadership. He suggested that he take 5% of his own founders' stock and set it aside. After a year Josh, alone, would decide whether either John or John was significantly more valuable to the company and, if so, Josh would award that person the stock. Otherwise, the stock would revert to Josh. This solution was totally at Josh's risk, and neither John nor John could object. It would take a potential inequity and make it fair. Both of them trusted Josh, his fairness and honesty. John and John agreed, the impasse was resolved, and part of Josh's stock was set aside.

* * *

With the hard issue of stock resolved, the founders moved on to find a company name. Ruttenberg had begun calling the company Newco, and the others adopted it to have a shorthand way of referring to what they were doing. No one thought Newco would stick, but they had tried using several other names and nothing had worked.

John and John wanted a space-age, star wars name, but Josh thought that was all wrong. He thought that VLIW technology, with its radically different approach to finding parallelism, was scary enough. He wanted a warm and fuzzy name to calm investors or, at least, a boring but solid name like Data General. He favored Elm City Supercomputer.

Over the months since they decided to start a company, they had tried out many names, quite seriously—using test names in documents. For a while they used Elico, for Yale, and it made the rounds in memos. Then as Sachem Computer, named for an Algonquian Indian Chief, they made a job offer to Bob Nix. Other recruits signed confidentiality agreements with the Elm Supercomputer Company. None of these names seemed right and with incorporation looming, the founders now needed to find a name that would stick.

They sat down together to find a name and then sat down again. And again. Josh was adamantly against star wars names.

"Let's name the company Mercury," suggested Ruttenberg. "The Mercury rocket took Apollo to the moon."

But Josh didn't like it, didn't like any of the Greek or Roman god names the others favored, thinking they were too derivative.

Ruttenberg vetoed regional names like Elico, Elm City and Sachem as tying them too firmly to Yale or New England. He always had eyes on bigger things, saw the company as the next DEC and wanted to make sure they didn't limit themselves.

By the time they sat down at our kitchen table in Woodbridge for one last try, blocking off the entire afternoon to work on the problem, they were veering slightly back toward space-age names. Josh had given up on warm and fuzzy and was now trying for a descriptive name, something that would reflect the technology. They tried several names involving flowing and oiliness—the logic dripping through the machine—and finally, Ruttenberg came up with Multiflow Computer. Josh liked it because he said it represented the instructions flowing through the code in many places at the same time, and it wasn't too scary. O'Donnell liked it too, and the three of them agreed. The company became Multiflow Computer.

Like all names, Multiflow got some strange reactions: "Is that an oil company?" "Does it make hydroelectric equipment?" "Please tell me the actual product will be sold under the Apollo name." Mark Brown, married to Josh's writing coach, Mary-Claire Van Leunen, said it sounded like "a high-tech toilet."

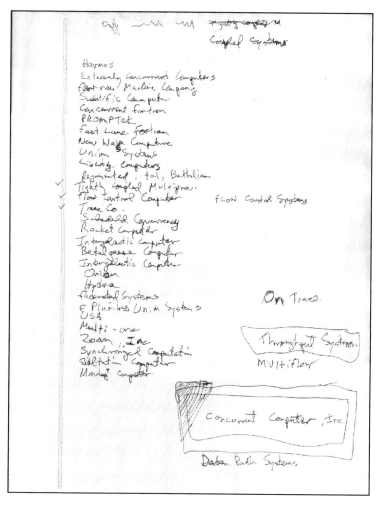

Brainstorming for a name at our kitchen table

MULTIFLOW COMPUTER

On April 3, 1984, less than two weeks after the founders met George Thibeault, Multiflow Computer was incorporated in Delaware, home to most of the Fortune 500 companies. The next week they borrowed $500,000 from Apollo and a week after that, Josh requested a two year leave of absence from Yale and ordered business cards for himself as President. He wanted to add CEO, but Ruttenberg told him that such grandeur was unseemly for a company as small as Multiflow.

They hired three employees who had accepted job offers; Bob Nix was the first employee to get a paycheck. Geoff Lowney joined, then Tom Karzes, Ben Cutler, and Nat Mishkin—all former Yale students, and they expected a lot more to join. New people started every week, sometimes more than one a week. The founders recruited everyone, interviewing friends, and friends of friends, and friends of friends of friends. When Josh tried to steal an administrator from Yale, Roger Shank told him that Yale was not his Little League.

"Not your 'farm team,' you mean," Josh corrected, and Roger became the first of many bosses to say that Josh was the most frustrating person he ever had working for him.

Bob Nix got the first Multiflow paycheck

With Multiflow taking shape, it was time for the founders to think concretely about a product—what form the VLIW computer would take. As an academic project the work had been theoretical, even when they were trying to build a working model. And when Josh and John approached manufacturers for a joint project the year before, they had only thought in terms of high-performance computers using the architecture and compiling technology. Now they and their partner, Apollo, had to think about size, pricing, actual performance, markets and the end-user. They needed a configuration, and they had to look beyond the academic world to what was happening in the industry—how Multiflow could have a part in it.

Today most technical applications run on powerful personal computers, with the few applications needing more power using supercomputers, but it wasn't always that way. As the mainframe computer era of the 1970s slid into the minicomputer era in the early 1980s, companies still maintained central control. Engineers in industrial manufacturing departments that needed a lot of power had to rely on booking time on central mainframe computers, competing with every other industrial department. They hated it, saying that dealing with corporate computer departments was as difficult as dealing with the IRS.

In the 1980s, scientific computing in industry was changing as departments started to buy their own minicomputers, but they longed for more power than they could get from these first minis. Mini-supercomputers, when they came on the scene, filled that need, and in 1983 they were the hot next product that everyone in the computer industry was talking about—individual departments would have computing power almost on the level of a supercomputer for less than $1 million. Thirty companies eventually sold mini-supercomputers; it was *the* exciting computer market niche of the 1980s, the place for a hot new technology. A VLIW computer would be a perfect fit, and the Multiflow founders decided that their product would be a mini-supercomputer.

* * *

On May 1, 1984, Multiflow signed a lease for temporary office space on Chapel Street near the Yale campus in New Haven. The office was small and on the second floor, but they expected permanent space to be ready long before they grew out of the temporary office. They bought very rudimentary computer equipment and used office furniture—big gray desks with plastic tops and old clunky chairs. And they began serious negotiations on the former telephone company garage in Branford, north of the Q bridge, everyone's choice for a permanent office. O'Donnell charmed the landlord who got caught up in the Multiflow romance: a new company, these young guys coming out of Yale, taking on the whole computer industry while working in his building. Like all vendors meeting with John, he came away with stars in his eyes, not able to do enough for Multiflow.

The company needed to hire a chief administrator, a really bright business person who could negotiate with landlords and with vendors for furniture, software licenses and supplies, someone who knew how to track the business plan, the engineering progress and the finances. It was great for O'Donnell to charm vendors but that wouldn't get the computer built. His time, and the other founders' time, needed to be freed for recruitment, technical management and the on-going Apollo negotiations.

I had been working on some of these first administrative issues—finding office space and employee benefits, but no one, me especially, thought this was a job I could handle. In the fall I was starting an MBA program at the University of New Haven where I hoped to pick up some of these skills, but at that point I didn't have them. And also, Multiflow was so small that, though I reported to Ruttenberg, it sometimes seemed as though I worked for my husband—and that didn't seem healthy. At home, Josh and I had always decided things jointly, and I didn't like how different things had to be at Multiflow. As leader, Josh was changing, becoming more decisive, a real executive, and my working with him in charge seemed claustrophobic.

When he and I first moved to Woodbridge we tried to maintain our egalitarian household, but it wasn't working. The previous year, as Multiflow took shape, I audited an early morning calculus class at Yale and three mornings a week Josh stayed home with both kids. But after Multiflow pitched into full gear, cooperation like that was impossible.

93

Josh now worked far harder than he had worked in his life and couldn't count on a reliable schedule—and all the household responsibilities fell to me. I missed working full time, but with my MBA program set to start I was happy to be able to spend time with the kids. Our lives in Darien were a cautionary tale of how things could go wrong when two people worked as hard as Multiflow needed them to work.

When no one at Multiflow knew anyone appropriate for the Chief Administrator job, Bob Nix went to friends at the Yale School of Organization and Management. They told him about Leigh Cagan, the best SOM graduate that year, a smart, really nice guy who was everything good you could say about someone you wanted to hire.

Leigh had always been interested in entrepreneurial ventures and, when he heard about Multiflow, he came and interviewed. Josh told him the story: the excitement of a revolutionary technology poised to take over the computer industry, the potential for great riches. It would grow big and fast; it had real momentum. Plus, since Multiflow was funded by Apollo and not by venture capital, it was far less risky than many start-ups—a great recruiting point.

The Chapel Street office was a big, open room on Leigh's first visit, with only two desks and four chairs. It didn't really look like a company, and Leigh was a little unsure as he sat facing Josh, knee to knee, during his interview.

"Leigh, you need to come back next Tuesday to meet the other founders." Josh said, "But when you come back, this office will be filled with desks. Leigh, every time you come back, while you are making up your mind, this company will have made a leap without you." Then, dramatically, "Don't let it make too many leaps without you."

That hooked Leigh, and before too long he accepted the job, becoming Badge 7 at Multiflow. And he was perfect for the job.

True to Josh's words, the Chapel Street office filled up quickly. Leigh bought a dozen used workstations from the defunct Canaan Computer Company at ten cents on the dollar, having been warned not to spend money like a drunken sailor.

"Although, I don't think that would be possible without a whorehouse next door," he said.

And he took the austerity program seriously, buying used equipment, close-outs and more bargains when companies went out of business, keeping a tight rein on Multiflow expenses. He introduced Lotus spreadsheets to run the business side of the company, making it all rational, bringing them the financial control they needed. PCs were new then, underpowered by today's standards, too slow for the engineers to use, but the state of the art at Yale's SOM, and Leigh brought the PC culture to Multiflow.

Leigh made administration effortless for the founders: so many things they didn't have to worry about, so many day-to-day concerns. He jumped right in, doing a lot himself—the same way the engineers did while building the computer. He was technical, understanding cars and stereos inside and out, and he wasn't afraid to tackle anything. He did every job that wasn't engineering—personnel, marketing and finance—until each job got so big it turned into a whole department with experienced people. And the industry veterans hired to replace him never did the job as well as Leigh had or with such good humor.

Early on Josh found Leigh in the hallway, after he had unclogged a toilet. He was waving the plunger manically in the air shouting, "Who ya gonna call?" after the 1980s movie, *Ghostbusters*. He fit right in.

Leigh Cagan - Who ya gonna call?

After a while Leigh got sick of saying "Multiflow employees" and looked for something more descriptive. Finally, he came up with "Multifloids" and the name stuck. Somehow, the "oid" sounded computer-ish to him, if a little dorky. The engineers took it up and so did the founders; they all called themselves Multifloids.

In August, Multiflow moved from Chapel Street in downtown New Haven to Branford, CT on the coast, to the converted telephone company warehouse. Chapel Street had become very crowded and now there would be offices to work in, closed offices. The new space even had a loading dock. They settled in, going full speed to develop the VLIW computer.

And the newly minted Multifloids threw themselves into their work: Nat and Bob Nix took over the operating system under O'Donnell's management, and Ruttenberg took over the compiler. Josh provided technical leadership, but he was too busy recruiting and getting the business off the ground to be involved on a day-to-day basis. He worked with the engineers when necessary, but mostly he left them alone. He respected them and had faith in their abilities. They were so smart that Josh let their creativity dictate how the machine would progress. Although the technology was based on his work, he was confident that their efforts would complement his.

The group thrived with this much freedom, everyone wanting to produce the best results, sharing the joy of scientific collaboration. They were working hard, working together, with people who were at the same genius level intelligence as they were, people who would be stars anywhere, with management completely behind them. It was fun and they trusted each other. There was the thrill of the hunt, of going unexplored places in architecture, the feeling of untrammeled space. They were getting to do what they wanted, build what they wanted, be part of a project they knew would make history. It was paradise for these smartest of engineers.

Some of the new recruits were shocked when Josh couldn't be as closely involved with the technology as they wanted, but since the engineering work was exciting, and the test results were starting to come in strong, they quickly adapted to the leadership structure. The engineers meshed, the new ones and those who had been part of the Tools Group at Yale. They became an unstoppable team.

It was easy to find the first technical recruits, software people from Yale and NYU, but it was harder to find hardware people since the founders' expertise and everyone they knew was in software. And New Haven was not Boston; it was "Silicon Nowhere," as Apollo and the VCs said, a place hard to entice people to move to. They made one hiring mistake early on, hiring a hardware engineer who was not up to the job and who ended up quitting. At that point, they went farther afield to the last reaches of their friendship networks looking for people to interview. And sometimes they found themselves talking to people very different from themselves.

There was one hardware recruit the founders ended up scaring. He was a stolid Midwesterner, a "white socks engineer," fashion challenged and socially awkward but, more importantly, although smart, only smart at engineering: someone who calculated his way out of every problem, not especially creative. They realized early in the interview that they wouldn't end up hiring him. His skills weren't right: creativity mattered in his job. And he didn't have the piercing intelligence they always looked for in the Multiflow crew. In another era he would have worn a pocket protector and carried a slide rule.

When given his choice of restaurants for lunch, the recruit picked a Japanese restaurant, to the founders' surprise. Because they weren't going to hire this guy, they didn't pay attention to the cultural mismatch they were setting up, but they really should have known better. Maybe the recruit was thinking of Benihana, a glamorous and fancy steak house—perhaps the only Japanese restaurant then available outside major cities. But this restaurant was not a steak house. It was an authentic eating place called Threshold and because of the spices the Multiflow founders, who ate there frequently, called it "Threshold of Pain."

When they got to the restaurant, the waiter asked them all what they wanted to drink.

"A milkshake," said the recruit and, to his amazement, found that a Japanese restaurant couldn't make him one.

The Multifloids were in the habit of asking the Threshold staff to make them whatever was good, not looking on the menu, and when the recruit didn't recognize anything on the menu, he was at a loss about what to order and went along with his hosts. That day there was a new appetizer the restaurant was trying out, and it turned out to be a plate of little wormlike pieces, standing up, waving. The recruit froze, horrified. He couldn't get out of the restaurant fast enough.

After that experience, the Multiflow founders realized that they needed a more reliable way to find good hardware engineers and turned to headhunters. They interviewed lots of people, clearly getting a better group of hardware recruits than they had been able to find on their own. They hired Dave Papworth and Paul Rodman from Prime, world-class engineers, worth their recruiters' fees many times over—as smart as any of the Yale software guys.

With twenty engineers and three administrative staff, Multiflow was set to go, churning full speed to a full-fledged VLIW computer design. Everyone worked long hours, sometimes staying all night. Enthusiasm and optimism were in the air. The results were terrific; they were on the road to success. They were going to revolutionize computing.

* * *

And then, in late August, the Apollo deal failed and all hell broke loose.

All spring and into the summer after Multiflow got the half-million dollar loan, they had continued to meet with Apollo, usually with George Thibault, but those meetings had slowed down. They had a term sheet and a memorandum of understanding with Apollo outlining the deal they had all agreed on, but no contract. Then, as the summer went on, the Multiflow founders had ignored how difficult it had become to reach anyone at Apollo; they were too busy getting the business going or, perhaps, pretending all was well. Yet, they did have misgivings. Ultimately, they couldn't ignore their uneasy feelings when Josh was summoned unexpectedly to an Apollo press conference on August 3 at the Boston Park Plaza Hotel. Suddenly, Poduska was out as CEO and a non-founder Josh didn't know, Tom Vanderslice, was in.

"This is going to be trouble," he thought.

The fear, the creeping dread, was unavoidable. Josh was afraid that Apollo, whom they were counting on for funding, had turned its back on them.

Bit by bit, word got to Josh that the Apollo founders, particularly Poduska, had soured on Multiflow, thinking that they were not living up to unstated terms of their agreement. Dave Nelson, VP for Engineering at Apollo and not Mike Greata, their usual contact, sat down with Josh in late August.

"The deal just isn't going to get done," he said. The momentum was gone: it had dragged out too long, they had lost Poduska's love and Poduska wasn't the CEO anymore anyway. The deal was dead.

The Apollo Board, at a time of management turmoil, had spent a precious hour discussing the Multiflow deal, with most of the founders wanting to terminate it. Ruttenberg told Josh that Vanderslice distrusted him because many years ago, as president of GTE, he had sold the consumer electronics business to Derald Ruttenberg, John's father. Then he noticed that Derald sold off many of the division's assets to finance his purchase. This is how a leveraged buyout works, but it seemed as though the senior Ruttenberg got something for nothing. Despite this and even though he was no friend of Multiflow, it was Vanderslice who spoke out in the Apollo board meeting against simply abandoning Multiflow, saying that in a small community like the computer industry, you couldn't treat people like that.

Because Vanderslice didn't want to leave them completely in the lurch, Apollo offered to buy Multiflow for a tiny fraction of the money in the original deal. The Multiflow debt to Apollo would be erased and the founders would receive several hundred thousand dollars each, but the twenty other employees would only receive a few tens of thousands of dollars each. This seemed perfectly reasonable to Apollo, even generous, but the Multiflow employees expected a greater reward, and people had relocated to Branford, CT with this in mind.

Josh thought that Multiflow was worth much more than Apollo was offering. With arrogant words he quickly came to regret, Josh turned Dave Nelson down.

"I don't think there is a single person at Multiflow who would want me to accept what you are offering," he said.

And with that, Multiflow was adrift without financing.

* * *

The situation was grim. Leigh immediately slowed payments to vendors, only paying the most necessary bills.

When Multiflow completely ran out of money in October, Ruttenberg loaned the company enough to pay for two weeks of employee salary. Then O'Donnell borrowed from his brother-in-law and bought them another two weeks.

"I know it's futile to throw my money away like this," he said. "Multiflow's sure to go under now, but I can't just sit by and do nothing, watching it die." He cared so much, not wanting it to end.

After the four weeks that O'Donnell and Ruttenberg's money bought, Multiflow ran out of cash again and this time there were no place to turn—Josh and I had no personal or family money to offer. Things were bleak and the founders discussed closing the doors. The situation looked impossible, as though there were no alternative to shutting down.

Payday rolled around and there were no checks. Then another payday and then another. Nat left right away to work at Apollo—that was why he was at Multiflow in the first place. But no one else quit, even when Multiflow finally ran completely out of money. They all felt the way O'Donnell had when he invested money he didn't have; they couldn't bear for it to go under.

Everyone knew how dire the future looked but they kept working, through six weeks without pay. Six weeks seemed like forever to Josh and me and to everyone else who went without pay and worked on. It couldn't last forever; everyone knew that. The technology licenses were expiring soon and, when that happened, development would close down. But through the fall 22 people worked in Branford, CT, at a company with no money, yet everyone kept at it.

Besides paychecks, Multiflow owed vendors for bills due well over sixty days, many for seventy-five days since Leigh had slowed payments months before. Luckily, the Apollo loan was a demand note with no specific repayment schedule—and no one was demanding repayment; otherwise they would have been out of business pretty quickly.

Leigh spent most of his time on the phone with vendors, trying to calm them down, so that no one would do anything extreme over an unpaid bill. O'Donnell, too, helped by getting vendors enthusiastic about the technology. Creditors came in, threatening to sue but, after talking to O'Donnell, they left wanting to give Multiflow even more credit; John's enthusiasm was infectious. But the weeks went on and Multiflow's unpaid bills piled up, until they reached $450,000.

* * *

Right after the Apollo deal failed, the founders got back in touch with the venture capitalists. Ruttenberg, especially, thought that Multiflow would have no trouble raising VC money since they now had a real company to sell, someplace investors could visit, no longer three guys and a car. Gene Petinelli of Fairfield Ventures had never really gone away, sniffing around every so often, saying that he was there if there were problems with the Apollo deal. Now he set up appointments with other VCs in New York, Stamford and Boston.

But it was rougher going than it had been during their first hopeful meetings a year earlier. Times had changed, gotten harder, and VCs were no longer funding anything that moved. This time it was mostly Josh, alone, who courted investors, talking to anyone who had any interest in Multiflow. He spent some time in Branford giving inspirational talks about his progress with the VCs and the quest for money, but most of his time was spent on the road. Since Josh had invented the technology, investors wanted to see him and to hear about it from the source. Presenting the company became his official role.

John and John had to stay in the office to manage the hardware and software efforts, getting the technical results needed to impress potential investors. And the intensity of O'Donnell's scientific vision scared investors; Josh was afraid to take him on the road. VCs saw him as a mad scientist, like Doc in *Back to the Future*. Presentations were a lot smoother when John stayed in Branford.

Josh went to meetings and more meetings. He haunted the offices of venture capitalists, some of whom thought "their money was greener than everyone else's." One of these was Nissan Boury, a cultured European representing a Rothschild fund. Ruttenberg was with Josh at this meeting because it was a family connection.

Boury, the aristocrat, was so clearly disdainful of them that Josh coldly terminated the interview.

"This meeting is clearly going nowhere," he said. "We shouldn't be wasting each other's time."

After they left, Ruttenberg turned to Josh.

"For me, as a human being, that felt wonderful," he said. "But it was a clear business low—and if you ever do it again, I'll kill you."

Mostly, though, the VCs were interested. And Josh went everywhere. He presented the company and the technology, selling everyone on Multiflow's potential for transforming the industry, talking about how fast the technology would run at low cost. And he had the research to back up his claims.

During a pivotal meeting in Boston, when Josh was giving a technical presentation in a conference room, a very nervous secretary broke in and handed Josh a message. John O'Donnell, who could convince anyone of anything, had convinced her that she had to interrupt this important meeting with the results of a technology trial the Multiflow engineers had just finished. This was a result of running an industry benchmark called LINPACK, and it was dramatic—better than Josh had expected. The Multiflow engineers had just run a simulation on a configuration they were confident would be better, producing faster results on compiled code. When the secretary handed Josh the note with the new numbers, it showed that the design would be indeed far faster on LINPACK, a real triumph. This was significant to everyone in the room; it created a dramatic moment when Josh introduced the new number at a critical point. It was so important that Josh kept that pink telephone message slip framed on his desk for many years.

The meetings continued, the VCs interested and encouraging, wanting to give Josh advice, but no immediate funding resulted. He worked closely with Gene and Felda Hardymon from Bessemer Venture Partners, and also people from Alex Brown Ventures, GE Venture Capital, Morgan Holland and from a lot of other firms. Few VCs ever turned Josh down directly when he asked for financing, but nothing concrete came of the meetings, even though Multiflow was a real company with impressive technical results. They said it was just a question of when they would invest, who else was part of the deal, and how they would do it.

"If this was easy, everyone would do it," said John Ruttenberg.

But it began to seem like foot-dragging. The VCs were afraid to commit, and Josh wondered if they were serious. Some of the venture capitalists began to talk to Josh about "personal guarantees," meaning that the VCs might lend money to the company with the founders guaranteeing repayment. Many entrepreneurs did this, took out what amounted to personal loans from VCs in order to finance their companies, but none of the founders thought this was appropriate. Ruttenberg had a family fortune to put at risk, and maybe this was what the VCs were after. For Josh it would be promising away his family's future; if Josh had agreed and Multiflow went bankrupt, we would go bankrupt, too. And, unlike Ruttenberg, our bankruptcy wouldn't do the VCs much good. Multiflow needed money on a scale that was outside anything that we would ever be able to repay.

After a few fruitless weeks of meetings, with the VCs being encouraging but vague when it came to specifics about money, Josh went back to Dave Nelson at Apollo. He tried to accept the buyout offer Apollo had made a few weeks before but Apollo was no longer willing. That offer had disappeared.

With things looking hopeless at Multiflow, Roger Shank the Yale Computer Science Chair took Josh to see Bart Giamatti, the University President. Roger wanted Josh back and he wanted him to hear it from Giamatti himself. Josh thanked them both and then did what he was doing wherever he went: he asked for money. He suggested to Giamatti that Yale should invest in Multiflow. But with an arrogance that reflected Josh's own when he turned down Apollo's buy-out offer, Giamatti refused.

"It is my sense of the Yale Corporation that they do not want me investing in computer start-ups," he said. And that was that.

Why didn't Josh go back to Yale when Multiflow's future seemed so grim? Any sensible person would have given up and taken the escape route back to Yale. Josh had planned to return, thinking this as recently as that spring, when Multiflow started. He loved being a Yale professor—and they wanted him back. So, why didn't he go back now? It really looked as though Multiflow wouldn't make it.

But the world had changed for Josh since Multiflow started, and his heart was irretrievably committed. Multiflow was now a real place with real people who were putting their careers and their futures on the line for his technology. Besides me and the kids, Multiflow was the emotional center of Josh's life; he felt about it the way he had felt about his extended family in his childhood. It never occurred to him to abandon the company when he could still do anything to save it.

It never occurred to Josh and it never occurred to me, either, to suggest that Josh leave Multiflow. I was pretty dazed then and scared. I didn't know what we should do, but I wanted Josh to do what he thought was right. Josh always put his family first, and his family now included the company. I couldn't imagine asking him to leave something he cared about as much as he cared about Multiflow. He could never abandon the people, and he couldn't abandon the chance for his scientific vision to be vindicated. He said that if Multiflow went out of business, he would be the one to turn out the lights.

* * *

After he had been visiting venture capitalists for a few weeks and not hearing any funding offers, Josh began to think hard about why this was happening. With all his experience winning over audiences, he could tell that they were responding to the content of his presentations. The technical results were convincing; the problem was somewhere else. He started to think that maybe it was him. To save his company, he needed to put his ego aside, to think about ways that he might be causing the problem.

When they first went to the VCs a year before, the three founders had planned to find an experienced CEO. They had interviewed several candidates. But when they accepted the Apollo deal and Multiflow was going to be a technology-only company, Josh decided he could lead it and they abandoned the CEO quest. Now it occurred to him that his lack of business background might be more of a problem than he realized. Maybe no one would put serious money into a company headed by him.

He asked the VCs what Multiflow would look like with a more experienced CEO, whether the company would have a better chance for funding. From the generally positive reaction, he decided that this was it. No one told him directly that his lack of experience was the problem, but Josh began to be convinced.

Where could he find an experienced CEO, though? No one he interviewed a year before had wanted the job; no one wanted to move to New Haven. And now it was impractical to move Multiflow to Boston. Josh had an established company in Branford, CT with lots of employees committed to it.

The VCs suggested going to a headhunter who specialized in finding executives for computer start-ups, Don Eckdahl. Before he became a headhunter, he had been a senior executive himself.

Don asked Josh to block out a whole day for him at Multiflow. They would meet in Branford and Don would learn about the company before trying to find them a CEO.

DON ECKDAHL

By this time in the Multiflow odyssey, Josh had met a
lot of senior executives but, when he sat down with Don, he
was startled. Don was nothing like the self-important,
pretentious people with social skills but no substance that
Josh was used to meeting. He was short, with a gruff
charm, low-key and unassuming. He was a real engineer—a
"white socks engineer"—with no polish, likeable and
easygoing. And he was very smart.

In November, 1984, Don had just turned 61. Three years
earlier he had retired as head of the computer division of
NCR but, when he found he didn't like the retired life in
Florida, he returned to work as a headhunter, setting up
operations in his home town, Los Angeles. He gravitated
toward computer start-ups because of experiences early in
his career.

As a Northrup engineer just out of school in the late
1940s, Don was part of a team that developed an early
computer to solve differential equations, replacing scores
of people using comptometers. He saw great potential in
his invention and flew it cross-country to be evaluated at
the Princeton Institute for Advanced Study by the great
mathematician, John Von Neumann. This was a delicate
operation in those early days, requiring him to buy an
airplane seat for the computer and to power it with
extension cords strung to an electric company across the

street from the Princeton Inn when their electricity proved inadequate.

Northrup was excited to use Don's computer to manufacture aircraft, but it didn't want to manufacture the machine itself as a product. In 1950, Don and two partners, with Northup's approval, started Computer Research Corporation to manufacture the digital analyzers. In 1953 NCR bought Don's company; it became their computer division, with him in charge. Don was behind NCR's rise to become a powerful force in the computer industry in the 1970s and 1980s. He also oversaw manufacturing for many years, establishing plants around the world. But when he didn't become CEO in the early 1980s at a time when he thought he should, he retired.

Now Don worked with young computer entrepreneurs, finding them key executives. When he started with a new client, he always described his early work, showing the founders of start-ups that he understood their problems. The implication was that if he were just younger, he would be in there with them, doing the same thing they were doing, because he had been there himself.

"I was born too early," he would say, telling the entrepreneurs that if he were working in a computer start-up now, he would get rich the way they surely would.

As Josh talked to Don, taking him through Multiflow's technology and operations, he began to look at him more closely. Don had real expertise in what a company needed to go forward, and he was very smart and a nice guy. It was obvious that he knew what he was talking about.

Multiflow needed a CEO; that was Josh's job right now, to find one so that his company wouldn't go out of business. Here, right in front of him, was a CEO, a real one, who knew what he was doing. And one who could be accepted by the company.

Don Eckdahl, 1984

"Hey," he said, "why don't you join us and be our CEO?"

"No," said Don, "I'm done with all that; I'll never do that again."

Josh looked at him harder and started to think. This would be ideal. Don could get them up and running fast, and time was important since a creditor could put them out of business any day. Even if Don wasn't a creative thinker like the Multifloids—he was a "white socks engineer," after all—Josh didn't think it would matter; Multiflow had more creativity than any company should need. Don hadn't said he didn't want to move to New Haven, or that he couldn't do the job. He just said no, reflexively. Maybe there was a chance; Josh was good at selling.

While Don was interviewing other people, learning about the company so that he could do a CEO search, Josh found John and John. He told them he was impressed with Don and thought he would be the right CEO for them; what did they think?

They had both spent some time with Don but not as much as Josh. They didn't have much of an impression but didn't hate the idea. They knew Multiflow was going under, and it seemed to them that going after Don was as good an idea as anything anyone else had suggested. So they told Josh to go ahead.

With the other founders' blessing, Josh launched his campaign to get Don. He went into selling mode, describing the excitement of the new technology, the sense of mission to change the industry, the thrill of working with his exceptional team—this group of employees so dedicated that no one quit when Multiflow ran out of money. And he described the potential for vast wealth. Don was reluctant, but he was listening.

Finally, Josh cut to the heart of Don's ego, to the way he presented himself, turning his own words against him.

"Well, okay, Don; but this is your chance." Josh said, " If you turn this down, you can never again say to anyone, 'I was born too early.'"

Don did not agree right away, but stayed another day in Branford to think about it. He saw enough value in Multiflow and its technology to make him think about taking this on, consider changing his life.

As Don thought it over, word spread through the company that "the old guy" was thinking of becoming their CEO. This was the best news anyone had had in a long time. They all knew how dire the financial straits were; no one had been paid in six weeks.

And as Don toured the company, with rumors flying, he could see how welcome he was. The warmth that greeted him was very seductive.

The next day, at age 61, Don agreed to take the job, move to Branford and become CEO of Multiflow. He was decades older than almost everyone else, taking on a company filled with people young enough to be his grandchildren. Ronald Reagan was president then, and everyone made comparisons.

* * *

Before Don went back to California, he met with key VCs from different venture firms to convince them he was serious, that he would move to Branford and lead the company. If the VCs doubted that Don had actually taken the job, there would be no money and Mutliflow would go out of business.

VCs who had worked with him before vouched for Don's seriousness and, based on that, the VCs loaned Multiflow $200,000 in seed money to keep them going until Don got started and they could get a round of financing together. The seed money didn't pay all of Multiflow's debts, but it paid back-salary and enough bills that vendors were no longer threatening to shut down the company. Everyone breathed a sigh of relief.

When Don arrived for work at Multiflow, everyone could see that he was different from them, different in culture and not highly educated like the engineers, many of whom had PhDs in computer science. When he moved into his office, he brought a fish with him, a mounted marlin he had caught. That marlin had hung on his wall at NCR and his office as a headhunter and now it hung on the wall behind his desk as CEO of Multiflow. It caused a lot of comment among the engineers, academics not used to sport fishing—they made detours to see it in his office. He was different, but they were glad he was there.

Don started as Multiflow CEO in January, 1985, with his highest priority being financing the company. The seed money gave them breathing space, but to get the product built, they needed serious money.

It turned out that Josh had been right: the VCs were waiting for Multiflow to have experienced management before investing. Now, they were ready to jump. But before the deal came together, there was a maneuver that VCs always did—something that they, gentlemen that they were, called "fuck you." It took weeks and it was excruciating.

Each VC tried to get as much of the deal as he could without squeezing everyone else to the point where the deal failed. If the deal was hot enough, the early people had the upper hand, but there was a lot of jockeying among early and new investors over what share of the company they would get. It was an elbowing out among colleagues with a lot of brinkmanship and very unpleasant. It was horrible, Multiflow afraid for its future since it had so nearly gone out of business. But the deal finally came together.

In February, 1985, six months after the Apollo deal failed, Multiflow closed on $7 million, its first round of financing. They had planned to raise $5 million but, with Don as CEO, the financing was oversubscribed. Even Apollo wanted in; instead of demanding repayment of its $500,000 loan, they rolled it into an investment. This touched even the VCs' hearts.

I was very startled to learn that closing on a company financing, with so much more money involved, is exactly like closing on a house. You sit in a room and sign hundreds of pieces of paper, your lawyer—George Thibault for Multiflow—by your side. Then checks get passed around but, somehow, you never see any money.

The final deal gave the outside investors 60% ownership of the company, leaving 40% to the founders and employees. Josh's original 40% of founders' stock, 20% of the company (since half the original stock had been reserved for employees) became 8%. Don nullified the hard-won compromise of Multiflow's incorporation, the 5% of Josh's founders' stock that had been set aside for John O'Donnell.

"That's ridiculous," he snorted and gave the stock back to Josh.

That took care of the stock but it also showed how Don intended to manage John O'Donnell—and Ruttenberg, too. The new Board of Directors included Don and Josh and three venture capitalists but neither Ruttenberg nor O'Donnell. At the closing they signed away this right, knowing what they were doing, knowing that this was the only way for Multiflow to be financed. They retained their proportionate share of founders' stock but they had less control, far less now than Josh did, and his was diminished, too.

When people asked Josh, and they often did, if it bothered him to "lose control of the company," he always answered that he never had control in the first place.

"When you start something like this, you lose control of the company ten ways from Sunday," he said. "You have to put your trust in the hands of other people, and any one of those people could be a total loser."

And asked whether he had to give up too much to get financed, now owning only 8% of Multiflow, Josh always said that owning a smaller part of a large business was far better than owning a large percent of something tiny. And a big percent of zero was still zero. It seemed like a good deal to him.

* * *

The weekend before Don started at Multiflow, he spent all day Saturday and Sunday working with Josh at our home in Woodbridge.

"Now, when are your weekly staff meetings?" he asked, first thing.

"Staff meetings?" said Josh, puzzled. "We're only twenty people. If we need to get together, we get together." Josh was getting the idea that with Don as CEO, Multiflow was going to be a very different place. And he wondered how the Multifloids would react.

As I watched Josh and Don working at my kitchen table, I wasn't worried about Multiflow's changing. I had just been through a terrifying period when the company nearly went out of business and I longed for stability—different sounded good. The bridge loan had been a respite, but it would take more normalcy for me to regain my confidence. The technology and all the people seemed solid, but the business backing looked shaky. As Josh and Don planned for the company to go forward, I hoped that it wasn't an illusion, that they really could make a go of it.

When Don started at Multiflow on Monday, the first thing he did was to ask Leigh to remove one out of every four fluorescent light bulbs in the office. Leigh did as he was ordered, but Josh thought this was crazy and asked what was going on.

"Appearances," Don said, "are very important."

It turned out that the VCs had told Don that he was going to have to keep a close eye on finances at Multiflow, that Josh's team was spending money like water. Don was reducing the lighting so that Multiflow would look like a company that was financially prudent.

"Whoa!" said Josh, "That's crazy. We're very careful with money," reacting not just to the strangeness of the light bulbs but to the unfounded accusation.

Then he learned that a major reason Multiflow couldn't get financing the year before was that Apollo had been bad-mouthing them. It was an Apollo article of faith that a start-up should never pay for a headhunter and Poduska had been outraged when Multiflow paid headhunter fees to recruit Dave Papworth and Paul Rodman. He thought it showed that Multiflow had no sense about money.

Josh was shocked. He had been racking his brains to figure out what went wrong with the Apollo deal, but this never occurred to him. The closest he could get to a theory was that having George Thibault as an attorney, someone who was legendary in the computer business, soured them on Multiflow. Maybe Apollo wanted a lower key deal than George's fire-power would allow.

He never thought anyone would think they were loose with money—particularly about something like this. Never mind how worthwhile the fees they paid for Rodman and Papworth had been, it seemed bizarre and self-destructive that Apollo was telling the VCs that Multiflow was irresponsible. At the very least, they had half a million dollars at stake if Multiflow went bankrupt—a demand note without even a repayment schedule.

"If you owe someone $20, that's your problem," he said, "but if you owe them that much money, it's their problem. What could they have been thinking?"

If Josh had known, he could have easily proved to the VCs that Multiflow was being careful, simply by producing the books. But the VCs hadn't asked; they had taken Apollo's words at face value. It became a key factor in the failure to get financing before Don came onboard.

After Don looked at the books and got to know the team, he realized how wrong it was to think the Multifloids were being financially loose. Leigh, with his Lotus spreadsheets, kept very tight control. With unlimited money, John O'Donnell might have spent freely, but Josh just had to convince him that they needed to spend time rather than money. At first that took some doing, because John would get brilliant ideas, which were actually brilliant, and rush headlong at them. But Josh knew that if they had any chance of holding the company together, they couldn't spend money on equipment it would be great to have. And once O'Donnell realized that he had to be careful, he came around. He used his incredible skill—he could do anything, and among the things he could do was spend less money.

And if the VCs had looked at the books when Apollo called Multiflow profligate spenders, they would have realized that Multiflow was vigilant with money.

* * *

After the first financing, Don hired people to fill parts of the company which had been missing when he joined, jobs the founders and Leigh had been doing themselves. He hired financial, manufacturing, and marketing people, finding employees more typical of a corporate environment. After a while Don was no longer older than everyone else by decades, no longer one of the few people without an advanced degree.

And Josh continued to be Multiflow's public face and couldn't lose himself in engineering. There were new investors now who needed to be kept up on what was happening. And they had partners who needed convincing; Josh had to provide a whole range of investor support for them to be willing to put money into a future round of financing. He went everywhere in those days, meeting with anyone who could advance the company and the technology. He came back to Branford for as many meetings as he could, but he was now back to spending a lot of his time on the road.

He traveled constantly. Sometimes he was merely "the entertainment" for star-studded events put on by VCs, impressive event following impressive event. After he spoke at a 1986 conference for Fairfield Ventures, Robert McNamara, the former defense secretary, gave him a lift to the airport so that he could fly to California for his next round of meetings. McNamara told him stories of his years at Ford and, like everyone at these conferences, told Josh how important innovation like his was to the future.

And it was always Josh going out and promoting the company. The product was going to be available soon and customers, as well as investors, needed to hear from the inventor before they would trust the technology, especially at this early stage. He was the one they wanted.

Whenever Josh was back in New Haven, I could always tell when he was on his way home because the phone calls started. In the half hour it took Josh to drive home from Branford, I had amassed a pile of messages for him, phone calls to return after dinner.

This was the time when I saw my husband turn into a senior executive. He looked the part already but in these years something else changed. No longer the contemplative graduate student, he became more focused and more decisive. If he wanted something, he asked for it straight out. If he had to say no, he didn't equivocate. He had to fire people sometimes and face the consequences of his actions. He did it, and then he went right back to work and handled the next challenge. He made decisions with an eye on the future, quick decisions, changing people's lives, involving millions of dollars. And then he had to go and do it again. I thought it was a dazzling change.

Don corrected one last thing about Josh's image. He told him he had to stop wearing his shirts straight from the clothes dryer.

"Permanent press isn't good enough," he said. "If you don't believe it, look at the next executive you see. Look and see whether the front placket is puckered. That is completely unacceptable."

So Josh looked and saw that Don was right; no executive has a puckered placket.

Embarrassed, Josh told Don that his wife wouldn't iron his shirts. But Don just laughed.

"No one's wife irons shirts any more," he said. "You have to get them professionally laundered."

Don and Josh on the cover of the Greater New Haven Business Digest

* * *

Three founders were too much for Don to deal with, especially since John and John were somewhat uncontrollable, given to wild flights of fancy. Josh drove Don crazy, being almost as unmanageable, but he was stuck with Josh who, after all, invented the technology. Don and the VCs hadn't wanted John and John on the Board and now Don ignored them. He thought their maverick style was dangerous and bad for the company's image, not what he wanted to project to investors and customers.

Don began to refer to Josh as "The Founder" of Multiflow. But Josh wouldn't stand for it and contradicted Don, even in public. Then Don switched, calling Josh the "Senior Founder," which he also hated. There was some justification to it, though, and Don told Josh it was good for the company. So Josh let it pass.

John and John really hated it, though, particularly Ruttenberg.

"What is this 'Senior Founder?' There's no role like that," he said, indignantly. "What does it mean? The three of us got together and started a company."

"Yes, the three of us got together and started a company. I don't like it either. You argue with Don; I've tried and I can't budge him," answered Josh.

But no one could argue with Don, and Josh became the "Senior Founder," providing him glory at the other founders' expense. This caused a rift that was very hard on Josh. John and John didn't think he was fighting hard enough. It was a tense thing among the three of them, painful for Josh.

Why did John and John stay at Multiflow when Don pushed them out of the way? If they left, their unvested stock would have vanished, but it seemed as though their pride would push them to leave anyway. But they couldn't leave, any more than Josh could leave when Multiflow was about to go out of business and Yale wanted him back. Multiflow had all of their hearts. It was the people, working as part of a world class team, what every engineer dreams of in a job: the sense of mission, being part of something they knew would succeed and change the world. That was what pulled at them, kept any of them from leaving.

* * *

During the first years after Don became CEO, Multiflow was golden. The hardware came back from the foundry and worked, the operating system was up and running quickly. There were no crises. No one quit. Multiflow looked like a well-run company, the kind of company that succeeds.

They did two more rounds of financing, closing on $10.6 million in May, 1986, and $18 million in May, 1987. The original venture capitalists subscribed proportionately and they let in a few new investors, including the Harvard Endowment. Yale had turned up its nose, not wanting to invest, but now Multiflow had Harvard. This was a far cry from the early days when Josh haunted the offices of venture capitalists. Multiflow was now a hot investment.

Just before the third financing, one of the VCs took Josh aside and told him, as a favor, that now was the time that he could "hold the company up." He was suggesting that Josh threaten to leave Multiflow unless he was allowed to liquidate some of his founders' stock in the financing, making us rich.

Josh thought about it for, maybe, thirty seconds. He pictured how he would face everyone, having threatened to bring down an organization they had dedicated their family's future to. These people who were almost as important to him now as his own family. Josh wanted to get rich but that wasn't how he wanted to do it. He would wait until it was time for the whole company to benefit.

When the second and third rounds of financing were coming together, Josh began talking in big numbers about our personal wealth, how rich we would be when Multiflow went public. As the negotiations went on, he would come home and say "we earned fourteen million dollars today" or "we lost seven million dollars today." At first, I got very excited or upset when our potential for wealth went up or down. After a while, though, the ups and downs were too much for me and I had a hard time listening to them. I found it too much of a roller coaster, our finances too unstable, for my peace of mind, and I didn't want to hear about it any more. Here was money, staring me in the face, and I didn't know how to deal with it.

The VCs were full of stories of computer millionaires, rich in this boom, who weren't used to money and put it in the bank, pretending it wasn't there. I didn't want to be like that, but I didn't know what else to do. My experience with affluence was limited to doctors and lawyers; I had never known anyone who was truly rich. I had no idea how they lived.

Ruttenberg was rich, of course, but I didn't know him well. He occasionally chartered a jet to fly from the tiny New Haven airport to his family's home in the Dominican Republic. And Margie Ruttenberg told me stories of going to charity galas at the Museum of Modern Art in New York, ending up touring the museum in evening clothes and bare feet. I scratched my head, but I couldn't see myself living this way. The scale was something I couldn't imagine.

When the Apollo deal was on the table, Josh had had dinner at Mike Greata's house—Mike had become very rich after Apollo went public, and Josh came home, talking about a strange household with live-in help and a lot of cars. Mike's wife would fill all the cars with gas, and Mike would drive one until it was nearly empty, then move on to the next car. This made no sense to me; I couldn't see myself doing any of that, either.

I finally decided that I should get contact lenses, since rich women didn't wear glasses—this was the limit to my imagination of wealth. I wore my lenses for a few years until they started bothering my eyes. When I stopped wearing them, I also stopped thinking about how I should live if I got rich. It was a high class problem to have—crazy to think I was worrying about it—and I figured time would solve it for me.

The years went on and the company grew bigger— seventy-five people, a hundred people, a hundred and twenty-five. Every year there were more and more kids at the company picnics, as the young engineers grew older, married and had children. Our kids grew bigger, too, and Multiflow was their reality. Our son Dave followed his father and became interested in computers, taking after school classes and going to computer camp in the summers. And the question of what to do with great wealth gradually faded away.

THE ENGINEERING TEAM

Bringing the product to market was now the most important activity, and this was Don's strength. From his decades of experience in the industry, he understood how to run a schedule, how to supervise activities and how to get a product out the door. There were schedule meetings every week, and Leigh kept track of progress on a white board, sliding a "today" marker he had rigged using a vertical wire attached with rubber bands. He had to re-write the board every six weeks since there was no commonly used project planning software then, following the schedule along with his marker between up-dates.

Don was far more controlling than Josh, whose style was hands-off. They made a good pair and they managed the company together, Josh mitigating the harsh effects of Don's iron fist and Don making sure things got done. The engineers looked to Josh to protect them from the corporate encroachment they were afraid Don embodied, but they knew that control was necessary to move the company forward. There were places where both sides had to give, tension between an Eckdahl-run company and a bunch of geniuses—the trick was to extract the most from each part. Don called the office "the plant," startling everyone with the hard core industrial term, but pretty soon everyone else called it "the plant," too.

Early on, the founders and Don had decided that the new computer would be called the Trace since trace scheduling was its driving principle. The machine they were building was inspired by the ELI-512 from Yale, but it was an entirely new machine, built completely from scratch. And they didn't want to use a name with Eli in it because it sounded regional, evoking Yale.

John O'Donnell had been working with VLIW concepts longer than any of the hardware engineers, so initially he was the one with the best overview of the computer they were building. Papworth and Rodman had built machines at Prime, but no one else in hardware had industrial experience. And many of the engineers were just out of school and had never done anything like this before, created anything as ambitious as a new machine. They were feeling their way along—all of them.

During Multiflow's first year O'Donnell, Papworth, and Rodman made all the high level Trace hardware design decisions—the backplane, the major data paths, the memory system, the floating point unit, and the integer unit. These were crucial decisions, the backplane most of all, because it was the skeleton of the system, complicated by a lot of boards, connections and pins. How it was set up determined how signals would travel from board to board—and getting it right was crucially important because once it was manufactured, it would be too expensive to change.

And while the hardware people were designing their part, the compiler people began writing the program that would use trace scheduling to tell the hardware which instructions to execute together. The first three: Ruttenberg, Geoff Lowney and Tom Karzes, had all been at Yale, and they modeled the Multiflow Compiler after Yale's Bulldog Compiler. They used the computer language C, but when it couldn't handle everything they wanted it to do, they enhanced the language, almost as if they were creating an entirely new one, adding structures the programmers could use—precise, elegant embellishments giving them more power to do what they wanted.

Geoff Lowney wrote the trace scheduler

Then, writing the compiler, each person handled something different—Tom the optimizer, Ruttenberg the back end and Geoff the trace scheduler. This is how large programs are usually created, and at Multiflow it was a good thing because each of the guys had radically different work styles—and very intense personalities. Ruttenberg could only plan out a program while he was writing and would correct his mistakes as he went. Tom, on the other hand, needed long periods of planning, making everyone edgy, but then would quickly write up flawless programs.

Tom could be intolerant of mistakes in other people's code, and mistakes were the natural byproduct of Ruttenberg's style of working. It was all the worse since Tom was so smart that he was usually right. Geoff was caught in the middle, reading the detailed public critiques Tom produced whenever he saw anything less than perfect—Geoff cringing as he got to his email every morning.

After a year Stefan Freudenberger joined the compiler group, a new PhD Geoff had recruited from NYU, and he added his focused relentlessness and methodical German precision to the mix. Stefan didn't work well with Tom's abrasiveness, even worse when you added Ruttenberg. He was so straight-laced that he told mild-mannered Geoff Lowney that he had to stop cursing or he couldn't work with him. And then Stefan had to work with the hardware guys—all strong personalities, too, and not given to moderate language.

The compiler group conflicts got heated and Josh wasn't sure what to do about them. In the face of the kind of pressure Multiflow was under and all the crazy personalities, he thought the natural thing would be to hunker down, to withdraw and push harder. It's what he would do—and O'Donnell, too.

But looking at situations in offbeat ways was Ruttenberg's strength. He had a different skill set from Josh or O'Donnell, and he used his unique view of the world to figure out how to create a team. He started holding weekly pizza lunches in his office to create a better working atmosphere—everyone in the compiler group required to go, no one permitted to discuss work for a whole hour. Josh and O'Donnell thought it was crazy when he told them about his solution. Pizza lunches? No work discussions? To solve a really hard work problem when they were under such work pressure? Only Ruttenberg could think that way.

But it worked; the compiler group became a more cohesive team—doing fun things together was just what that crew needed; it created an underpinning of trust. They found that Stefan had a silly side and a great sense of humor, and all of them put aside their egos and their work style differences. They began enjoying each other's company and turned their intensely focused personalities toward getting the compiler written, ignoring the occasional clashes because of their new-found camaraderie.

With product development in full gear, Multiflow added as many stellar people as it could find: Chris Ryland, Woody Lichtenstein, and many others—hiring first rate computer scientists to do engineering. Anyone who didn't want to join permanently could be a consultant—the combination was synergistic. It was all fine with Multiflow; they just wanted the best people and they took them any way they could—setting them loose to work on hard problems building the Trace.

Woody joined from Culler Computer to work on the compiler and the operating system, but he branched out since he had such wide-ranging interests. Like the other Multifloids, Woody was super-smart and could do anything—nice, very decent, and fun to be around. Multiflow was so loose in its organizational structure that at one point he and John Ruttenberg reported to each other on different aspects of the work. And Woody was surprised to find himself learning from the Multifloids in areas where he thought he was an expert—software engineering from Ruttenberg, performance analysis from Geoff and ordering rational numbers from Tom Karzes. And Tom, with his abrasive style, taught Woody about referring to people who didn't measure up to his standards as "a real waste of water and minerals"—the composition of the human body.

The engineers handled most of the technical recruiting, but every so often Josh got involved when there were problems—and sometimes they drew me in, too. When a recruit's reluctant wife needed convincing that Multiflow was a real business or that Connecticut was a good place to live, I went to dinners or on trips, playing "executive wife," a role I never had to fill before. I found this strange and a bit uncomfortable, but I could see that the wives I met wanted to talk to a woman, so I stepped in when I was needed. Josh had never wanted to be a business executive and I never wanted a life confined to being "the wife," yet here we were playing these roles—me in the supporting position.

In late September, 1985, Josh and I flew to Houston to interview a finishing Rice PhD, who had special skills and a wife who didn't want to move to Connecticut. Two days before our trip, Hurricane Gloria made landfall near us on the coast and wiped out our electricity and that of the entire New Haven area. The kids thought the whole thing was fun and were thrilled when we decided to go anyway because that meant that Leigh and his wife Christine, the kids' favorite people, would come to stay with them, stepping in as we had planned, their house as dark as ours from Hurricane Gloria.

I tried my best during our trip to Houston and so did Josh, both of us striving to look like the ideal executive couple; I was learning to put on a persona I didn't feel. But it didn't go well, and I couldn't sell Connecticut—she didn't like that it was all so old, the recruit's wife said. I didn't know what to say in response, and I worried that a "real" executive wife would have had something more to say.

Multiflow didn't get the guy from Rice, but others were eager to join. Bob Colwell, a hardware guy, came to Multiflow, defying expectations that he would go to Intel since he had spent his summers working there.

As a Carnegie PhD student, Bob had been interested in the same problem Josh was, the need to hand-produce horizontal code. He had heard Josh describe VLIW technology, but it sounded ridiculous to him then—he wasn't sold on compensation code, the additional code trace scheduling adds when its first guess path is wrong. But since VLIW spoke to his interests, he gave it a lot of thought. Then he got a call from Paul Rodman, who had been a graduate student with him—they designed a digital music synthesizer together.

"Hey, we're doing this really cool start-up—we're building Fisher's crazy machine. You're graduating; come on up and join us," said Paul.

"Oh, Geez," thought Colwell. "Do I really want to bet my career that there's something here?"

Bob Colwell and Paul Rodman, 1985

But he went to Branford and interviewed—and liked what he saw. When he met Dave Papworth and spent time with him, he realized that Dave knew what he was doing—and had reason to think VLIW was going to work. And he looked around the company and liked the culture, too. Dave was a notorious eccentric, reputed to never have bought furniture for his house in Branford. And once Dave, famously, went home one weekend and took his late-model Corvette engine apart—into little pieces on the ground—and put it back together so that it worked.

So Bob took the plunge. As a bonus for the company when Bob joined, Multiflow also hired his wife, Ellen, a compiler writer.

And Rich Lethin joined after finishing his undergraduate degree at Yale. He had taken Josh's architecture class in 1984, the year John O'Donnell was Teaching Assistant and co-instructor, and caught the VLIW bug. He was excited by all the cutting edge computers they studied in the class, O'Donnell pouring out material with the velocity of a fire hose—and all of it was colored by Josh's passion for his research.

Rich was younger than the other Yalies, too young to have known many in the Tools Group, but he remembered that class. After he graduated he interviewed at IBM and a few other places, but decided that Multiflow would be the most fun. He stayed a few years and then left to get his PhD at MIT—returning to Multiflow several times along the way. He was so slight and blond that I thought he looked too young to be an engineer. But he plunged right in.

As a new graduate with only a bachelor's degree, Rich was assigned to do the lowest level of engineering, hired as a glorified technician. Everyone assumed he would be a bright kid helping out in the lab who would pick up "real engineering" over the first year or two. But to the amazement of the engineers, he instantly became one of the best, with a broad grasp of architecture, software, and electronic details that would have been exceptional in someone with ten years experience.

He was very young, though—and showed his youth occasionally. When he accompanied the first machine Multiflow sold, the beta machine sent to the Supercomputer Research Center, he got bored staying in Washington, DC for the weeks it took until everyone was convinced that it performed the way it should. He decided to test the machine, to stress it in ways it wasn't designed to run—something better done in Branford. The machine crashed, blowing away its operating system, and Bob Nix had to fly down to help Rich reinstall it.

When Rich was hired, he had the idea that he would be starting at nine in the morning and leaving around 5pm. On his second day he met an administrator in the hall on his way home, surprised he was leaving that soon.

Rich Lethin working on a board

"Hey, you're heading home at five o'clock?" she asked.

"Well, um, yes... It's the end of the workday, right?" he said.

"Well," she said, "I'm not sure..."

So the next day Rich decided to figure out how late people actually worked—and was amazed at the hours people spent in the lab. He started doing it, too, then, working long hours with everyone else, taking very few vacation days. And he started feeling the creative energy at Multiflow. He could work with Dave Papworth on the floating point board until 2am then finally call it quits—leaving Papworth behind him in the lab. Then he'd get in at 10am the next day and work until 4am. And it went on like that for three years, working seven days a week.

Rich had a girlfriend from college who kept wondering where he was. She'd see him, and then he'd disappear for a few weeks and then reappear and they'd take a walk before he headed into work on the weekend. Most of the married guys were more balanced: Ruttenberg, Geoff, and Bob Colwell, but they worked long hours too. For about six months, Bob Colwell rarely made it home for dinner. His wife, Ellen, now part-time after the Colwells' second child was born, brought Bob's dinner—and the kids—to Multiflow many nights each week, since this was the only way they got to have time together as a family. When Bob finally got home, as often as not he continued working at the terminal next to his bed—designing or debugging. He went to sleep and when a routine finished, the terminal beeped and woke him. He typed in the next thing and went back to sleep, never really leaving the job.

When Ellen and Bob first joined Multiflow years earlier, they had had a hard time finding childcare for their first child who was then a baby—reminiscent of the childcare problems Josh and I had had in Darien. Geoff, whom she reported to, was in a hurry for Ellen to start, though, and suggested that she bring the baby to Multiflow with her while they was still interviewing nannies. He set up a separate room for the two of them, and it worked for a while. But one day, with a Board of Directors on-site meeting scheduled, Don came to call. He cooed over the baby, but after he left, he turned to John Ruttenberg whom he brought with him.

"Get that baby out of here!" he ordered. And that arrangement fell apart.

When Ellen had her second child while working at Multiflow, no one knew how to handle it. As a small company with few women, they had no maternity policy, but wanted to be competitive.

"Go home, have your baby—we'll just keep paying you," said Geoff. This was what they had decided on. And it put a lot of pressure on Ellen, who came back to work as fast as she could, leaving both kids with a neighbor, later switching to part time work.

But despite not accommodating a baby, Multiflow was mostly an informal, unstructured workplace, and people liked working there. John Ruttenberg led bicycle groups at lunch around Branford and the surrounding towns, to beautiful spots like the Thimble Islands. Going with him was a popular outing, extending far beyond the compiler group, Rich commonly joining in. And Rich kept his windsurfer strapped to his car and watched the wind, waiting for it to be perfect. When it was right, he would leave work and windsurf for a few hours, glad for Multiflow's location on the Connecticut coast.

As Rich worked, he wondered how Josh got all these amazing people to join Multiflow. This was one of the things he prized most: the opportunity to have colleagues like he never imagined he could have. I wondered the same thing, but when I asked Josh he had no real answer. He said it wasn't all him, that once great people started joining, they attracted people as good as they were. And that the company had the right stuff—the technology had the right stuff and that everyone wanted the thrill of working with an exciting new technology. And that he was good at selling people on all of this.

But I believed it was more than that. Josh was impressive, logical and smart—and reeked of integrity. I thought that these qualities—what was special about him—were what attracted so many extraordinary people to Multiflow.

It was a great group, better even than Josh's group at Yale had been because it was so much bigger. And they were compatible, despite their strong personalities. There were no prima donnas. How could you be a prima donna when Dave Papworth was around? Maybe, if you were Paul Rodman, but Paul was too steady for that. They were all like that—Ryland, Colwell, Papworth and the others: easy going, high energy, hard working, hard driving and fun—joking and enjoying their work.

They were perfectionists about their work, too. Someone outside the company told Josh that any time a Multifloid gave a presentation, he refocused the slide projector, unwilling to accept focus that was good enough for people from other companies. Josh watched at presentations and saw that it was true. Only the Multifloids refocused. And he did it, too—a Multifloid, changing the projector focus every time he gave a talk.

And all the engineers worked together, too, not respecting the traditional computer science boundaries—no areas were off-limits. The software and the hardware were co-designed, each group influencing the other. For classically trained computer scientists, crossing boundaries between hardware and software might seem fraught. But engineering, unlike mathematics, is a team effort, and this collaborative, interdisciplinary approach increased the company's effectiveness.

Some of the Multiflow crew—hardware and technical support

Everyone had his individual piece, but they shared and consulted. Hardware guys stuck their noses into software and the software guys meddled back. When the compiler guys hit a crunch, they pulled in Bob Nix from the operating system group to port the UNIX Fortran compiler, a crucial part, since so much of scientific computing was written in that language. Chris Ryland, Doug Gilmore and some of the others from the operating systems partially rewrote the math library. And John O'Donnell could implement software after talking about it for only an hour.

Geoff was amazed to see how people would rise to the challenge when given the chance. Of the compiler guys, only Tom Karzes had industrial experience, and that was just a year at DEC following his undergraduate work. But they all had so much flexibility and breadth that anyone could pitch in and do anything. Bob Colwell, a hardware guy, shared an office with Stefan Freudenberger, a compiler guy. The offices were so small and the desks were so close that if Bob leaned back, Stefan had to sit straight up in his chair. And if Bob had a compiler question he would just ask. Rodman, too, and especially Dave Papworth, hardware guys, would put their de-bug hats on and barge around wherever the clues took them—they were fearless. And so was everyone else. It was the company culture.

BUILDING THE TRACE

When Josh invented VLIW technology, he thought the hardware would be easy to build—that trace scheduling was the hard part. But the sheer quantity of instructions executed together was a problem—the "very" in VLIW. Because the instruction words were so much wider than in any other computer, with more operations executed at the same time, everything was complicated and they ran into trouble. They were pushing the limits of what hardware was designed to do, and achieving computer cycle time goals was difficult, time consuming and expensive.

As with any computer, there were so many places where any single fault on a solder joint could do them in. But on the Trace, there were so many more solder joints, components, parts, and integrated circuits than on other computers—all being used to the margin. If any one of them was defective or simply overheated from being too crowded together with other parts, everything got thrown off. And it would take days to figure out what was wrong—pushing them farther behind schedule.

Luckily, the hardware framework O'Donnell, Papworth, and Rodman set down that first year held: the back plane, the data paths, the memory system and the rest. Because they had made the right decisions at the beginning, the hardware people could fill in the blanks and design the boards, relying on that structure.

It was a battle to make a reliable machine and they became expert—Bob Colwell, Dave Papworth, Paul Rodman and the rest of them, spending entirely too much of their time debugging. They personally went over each of the first machines Multiflow produced and hand modified a lot of them until the product was out of the "art" stage. Then they could train the manufacturing people to do the job themselves—correcting the mechanical errors that came back from the fabricator.

The chip in the center of each board drove the clock and, heavily loaded, it got overheated and malfunctioned—there was a false tick, a murmur, that the computer would misinterpret, throwing everything off. These were the "ground bounce demons" that Bob Colwell was always chasing, electricity bouncing around, causing malfunctions. When things like this happened, John O'Donnell mostly stayed out of the hardware guys' way, but when problems cropped up with the central chip, he tried grappling with circuits pushed beyond their limits. In desperation, John insisted that they solder a layer of shielding over the chip, thinking it would help. It didn't seem to, though, and Dave Papworth derisively called John's shielding—which he continued to insist on—a "magic talisman," the height of insult at scientific Multiflow.

Boards in the computer cabinet overheated, too, because things were crammed together, everything pushed to the limit. They used cold spray to identify some of their problems with overheating, buying cans of compressed air by the case; when they sprayed it on overheated components and the problem went away, they knew where to look for the culprit. But the power supplies kept smoking and burning out, destroying thousands of dollars of chips in the process. The Multifloids called this problem "flaming power supplies," although they really just smoked, never flamed. To fix it, Rich got the schematics from the company that made the power supplies and spent a couple of days figuring out different ways to wire them together— stopping the overheating problem on those components.

They used a rubber mallet to seat the pins in the back plane, hitting all the pins for good measure. That mallet acquired mythic status, and as Rich used it, he was alarmed to realize that he was pounding—whaling away— on boards each of which was worth more than the car he was driving. All the boards got pounded like this and then run in a hot box to stress them—thousands of dollars worth of components.

And Paul Rodman learned how to make the Trace sing— literally. When the computer was working hard, the power supply made a tone, a different one depending on that it was doing. When it did repetitive computations in a loop,

Paul Rodman building the Trace

141

the tone was sustained as long as the loop continued—at whatever tone the computation produced. Paul wrote programs using loops at different levels of intensity, making the machine play tunes as it worked.

The process got smoother as time went on, but each machine had to be stressed before it was shipped and when any computer malfunctioned, the problem had to be traced back. To help with debugging, Rich wrote a program to randomly test each computer before it was shipped, exercising all the logic circuits intensely and in parallel, the program written in such small pieces that when it ran, it was easier to pinpoint the problems. They no longer needed days to trace problems back; everyone's life got easier.

Bob Colwell designed the global control board, the heart of the system—the last board to be designed. They had been putting off designing it, and before Bob joined, everyone worked around it, avoiding everything they didn't understand, pushing all those functions onto that board.

"Oh... The GC will take care of that," they said. And a lot of "that" had no documentation.

Building the GC board was a daunting job, but Bob, unfazed, set about it. Using systematic analysis and, like a chemist or a biologist, keeping the results of his experiments in beautifully illustrated notebooks, he built the GC with its laundry list of requirements.

He personally debugged the first 43 global control boards, a heroic effort, and the third one manufactured, GC#3, was a particular problem. It malfunctioned when it arrived from the fabricator, and Bob worked on it for weeks, modifying the board so that it booted reliably and ran the operating system. When he finally got it up, it was so jury-rigged, with wires everywhere, that plugging it into the system might cause it to break—or break something else. He stored it in his office so that it wouldn't accidentally get shipped to a customer and ruin Multiflow's reputation for quality.

But the Vice President of Manufacturing hired by Don, didn't agree with Bob Colwell's assessment. He came into his office and asked if he knew where GC#3 was.

"That board's inner layers were too etched during manufacturing," replied Bob. "If you flex the corners, you can still cause the inner layer traces to break. That board will never be reliable enough to ship. We'll just keep it here for system testing."

The VP's face turned a strange shade of red. "That's not your call to make," he said. "It's mine—and I say we ship that board."

Bob Colwell was outraged, thinking the industry veteran was incompetent and had no business at a start-up. He certainly didn't share Bob's standards.

"I'll look for GC#3," he said, "and if I find it, I'll let you know." After the VP left, Bob put GC#3 behind his desk; it never got shipped to a customer.

As soon as the Trace was up and running enough to be reasonably reliable in the lab, John O'Donnell made the business decision that all work from now on had to be done on the Trace. They had been working on a Pyramid, a high performance minicomputer, one of the first using the UNIX operating system. Multiflow used the Pyramid so that they could build on a system as similar as possible to the one they were designing; they had decided to use UNIX in the Trace after the Apollo deal failed and they moved away from Apollo's proprietary operating system.

In this same spirit, John thought they had to "eat their own dog food"—believe in their own product enough to use it themselves. Over a weekend John made the switch, moving everyone's files to the Trace and turning the Pyramid off permanently.

The engineers thought O'Donnell was nuts since the Trace was barely working—they were afraid they wouldn't be able to get anything done. Pretty soon, though, the engineers adapted, and John was right. The Trace ended up being a better product because they were forced to use it—and could see where the problems really were. The compiler people strung wires from their offices through the heating vents to the hardware lab to get better access to the Trace, since easy networking was years in the future. Everyone got used to working with cobwebs of electrical cords strung everywhere, long straggly things. It was all part of the clutter.

A real problem cropped up when the CPU team was designing the register chip, the place the computer stores the data it is working on at the moment. The design was for one big set of registers on a chip, accessible by both units that did integer arithmetic. Because the Trace needed so much to be done at the same time, the chips were always crowded, and fitting everything in was a problem—the greatest tension in the design. And on the night before the deadline to ship the register chip design to the fabricator, the CPU team was having trouble. The whole register fit on the chip—but not so both integer units could access the whole thing.

As the team worked, they rearranged it and rearranged it, being careful not to affect the architecture—but they just couldn't get it to work. And they had to ship it that night; the deadline at the fabricator was the next morning. If they missed it, they would miss their manufacturing slot and the product would be behind—a serious matter in the competitive mini-supercomputer market.

On this particular night there were no compiler people in the office to consult, and because it was so late, they knew they would wake people up if they called anyone. Finally, with the deadline approaching, the CPU engineers made a decision themselves, trying as best they could to have minimal effect on performance. They split the register in two, attaching each side of the chip to only one of the functional units, confident that they were making the best choice. The only alternatives they saw were to slow the machine down or not ship the design that night and miss their fabrication slot, delaying the product—neither of which they wanted to do. So they changed the architecture to make the integer arithmetic units access each side individually. They created the split brain problem.

The next morning there was a real uproar when the rest of the engineers found out about the architectural change the CPU people had made the night before. It was irrevocable—the design was shipped; it was in silicon now. The hardware guys said there was nothing else they could have done and it didn't affect performance much, only one function. This was correct, but the software guys weren't so sure the hardware people had made the right decision. The extra instructions used to move the data from one half of the register file to the other might offset the gains trace scheduling provided.

And Josh was appalled. The whole idea of trace scheduling was for the compiler to look at all the code at once. VLIW needed rich connectivity; he had even wanted full cross-bars so that all the register banks could be connected, even if it came at the expense of some performance. A split brain was entirely wrong; in his mind the CPU guys' choice violated the conceptual model of the technology. Josh wished so much that they had called the compiler guys the night before for advice, middle of the night or not. He believed that the compiler people wouldn't have allowed the decision to go the way it had, and he was horrified that the computer's brain had been split, even to this small extent.

But what would have happened if the CPU guys had waked up Ruttenberg or Lowney and asked for their advice? There was no quick solution or the CPU guys would have seen it. If they had delayed, they would have missed their fabrication slot and held up the product. And Josh didn't want that—the CPU work would have ground to a halt. And maybe there was no other way of designing the register chips. Maybe the split brain problem was inevitable, as the CPU guys said.

Ruttenberg agonized over the problem, and the compiler group rose to the occasion, reengineering the compiler around the problem. And in the end there was minimal impact, although it was a real disappointment. Whenever Josh thought about the split brain, he realized that it just showed how hard the hardware/software partnership was. Working at the boundary of architecture and compiling, even hardware engineers with the best will possible, who co-designed their hardware with the software guys, could make a decision threatening the spirit of the technology.

* * *

As he watched the engineering team building the Trace, Josh was haunted by thoughts that it was all too good to be true. It wasn't that he doubted the Multifloids' abilities, their amazing intelligence or dedication. The problem was that he remembered the skeptics in the industry who said that a VLIW computer couldn't be built, and in Josh's darkest moments he was afraid that it might be true. When problems like the split brain cropped up, he worried his fears might be realized, that it was all a lot of fun—the Hardy Boys building a computer—but that when the hardware came back from the fabricator, there would be a horror show. It would never work and Multiflow would go out of business.

These were doubts that he shared with no one—not even me—black thoughts which haunted him. Some darkness inside him was taking over, no matter how cheerful and optimistic he seemed on the outside. He was very upset.

I knew something was wrong, but it was hard for me to tell exactly what—I thought it was the pressure he was under, the travel schedule and how tired he was. I didn't know the worst of it—the roller coaster of his emotions—how worried he was about the future of the company.

On the contrary, I had always believed in Josh's technology, even from the very first. Now, with all these first-rate engineers signed on and money from VC financing, I didn't think they could lose. Because Josh was not sharing his fears, I didn't know how deeply the skeptics in the industry had scared him. That he heard echoes from his youth telling him that his learning style would prevent him from being successful, saying that he had messed up again, letting down everyone who was counting on him.

But, in a flash that stunned Josh, when the Trace came back from the fabricator, it worked—right out of the box. It still needed debugging, but they plugged the boards into the chassis, and the machine worked—with no logical errors. The engineers installed a rudimentary operating system and it, too, worked perfectly. The adders did addition; the registers stored data; the different parts of the computer communicated—just like it was supposed to. Then they got UNIX, the real operating system, ported to it in no time—also working perfectly.

Josh couldn't believe it. He had had so many doubts, but now the machine was working—correctly.

But then the roller coaster of his emotions crashed to the ground again when they started running application programs and the performance was terrible. Correct, but very slow—truly horrible. Twelve times slower than it needed to be to be commercially viable. Josh thought all his fears were confirmed. They weren't in business to build machines that only worked correctly; they needed the Trace to go fast and it wasn't happening. Josh thought that it was all a mess and no one would ever buy a computer that ran like this.

To work on this problem, Multiflow declared an all-hands-on-deck emergency, dedicating any loose resource to the performance problem—and a lot that weren't loose, too. There was a lot the engineers could do, standard industry tricks—mostly modifying the compiler since it was so much easier to change than the hardware. There were optimizations like strength reduction (such as adding a number to itself instead of multiplying by two), operating system efficiency issues, memory hierarchy issues, cache system issues, buses that stopped when they weren't supposed to—40 or 50 things on the list. They put together a plan of attack and began having weekly performance meetings, replacing the schedule meetings, since performance was so much more urgent now. It was all supposed to work—science said so.

Bob Nix, head of the operating systems group, led the performance meetings, along with John O'Donnell, because Nix was organizationally neutral, not part of either hardware or compiler, both places where performance comes from. And Bob was one of the most analytical of the bunch, with the mathematical nature needed for the job. Josh helped with analysis and decision making, while Don mostly stood to the side, and the engineering teams implemented everything that came out of the meetings.

The Multifloids expected all the tricks to work, getting performance speed-up of a factor of two here, a factor of three there. And you multiply the performance factors when the problems are independent, getting far higher performance when the tricks were used in combination.

But Josh looked at it and rolled his eyes, still with dark fears and deep misgivings he didn't share with anyone.

"Look," he said to himself, "I'm a scientist, but I'm also a human being. It isn't going to work like that. The thing that's supposed to be twice as fast is going to be 1.05 times as fast and the thing that's supposed to be three times as fast is going to be 1.16 times as fast. It just isn't going to work."

Despite the army of super-bright engineers and having science on his side, the inner skeptic was dominating the scientist. And it scared him—badly.

The performance war pulled everyone at Multiflow together; it was a brotherhood of soldiers in a fight—a company-wide challenge. This time even Stefan and Tom Karzes let everyone—mere mortals—muck with the compiler more fully than they had before. And they did it mostly with good grace, although at one point Tom threw a sandwich at someone in a fit of pique.

It was too tense for Josh to enjoy, but the rest of the Multifloids turned out like gladiators launching a war, gleefully pushing against what the machine could do. And it was satisfying to see their achievements. There was a number—this week's performance measured against last week's. It was like an Olympic event, the most intense work experience of any of their lives.

And Multiflow fixed the Trace's performance. Everything worked—just the way science said it should.

The machine began going blazingly fast, just as Josh's research said it should.

It turned out that when they designed the computer, they focused their efforts almost exclusively on the hard mathematical parts of performance—the parts their competitors had trouble with—and neglected many of the more visible, easier aspects of performance. For instance, when they demonstrated an early Trace to an oil exploration company which used simulation software, the exploration calculation ran perfectly—the hard mathematical part that had stymied other computers this company considered buying. But when the Trace tried to draw the result of its calculations, it was truly terrible—drawing the result painfully slowly, as slow as a Prime minicomputer.

To fix these more externally visible aspects of performance, they hired Cindy Collins, an expert in these areas. She was a strong-minded woman, strong enough to stand up to the intense Multiflow personalities without any benefit of sisterhood to back her up, now that Ellen was part-time. She solved a lot of the problems, and the guys found more—the Fortran compiler, the math library and several others which they continued to work on for years.

But they were over the hump; they could see their way to the performance the technology promised. Every trick they tried produced the result it was supposed to produce. Every week the Trace was going faster. The theory worked—Murphy's Law was on vacation. They finally had a machine they could proudly show to customers.

And as Josh watched, he thought it was the most remarkable thing he had ever seen. He didn't relax; he was too busy for that. But he began to realize that the Hardy Boys could build a computer after all.

PRODUCT INTRODUCTION

The Trace Computer

On April 21, 1987, the Multiflow Trace debuted to the press at a glittering event at Windows on the World in New York City. A Trace stood on a platform in the middle of the room surrounded by the press and analysts and by Multifloids, their families and friends. The restaurant, on the 106th and 107th floors of the North Tower of the World Trade Center, later destroyed in the 9/11 attacks, looked over all of New York City. It was gorgeous, decorated with beautiful, sculptural bouquets of tiger lilies, then rare in business settings. The product launch was a glamorous, sparkling evening, everything you could want for your company to succeed.

Before the product introduction, three beta sites took Traces: Sikorsky Aircraft, Grumman, and the Supercomputer Research Center, part of the National Security Agency. The beta site companies bought early products at below-market prices in exchange for providing feedback on the product's performance.

At the product introduction, each site presented a report—and they were glowing.

"...faster, cheaper and easier to use than anything on the market."

"Not only do you have a reasonably priced supercomputer, but you don't have to rewrite software significantly."

"Within two hours of uncrating, it was up and running."

"I wish I could ever get a product from DEC or IBM that was as polished as this."

The founders toasting the Trace, ready to ship

The vibe was great and that night Multiflow looked like everything you wanted a start-up to be: glamorous, nuts & bolts, successful, the next big thing. Customers and analysts stood up and talked about the product, giving speeches lavish with praise, predicting a glorious future.

The Trace was a remarkable product, as everyone said, polished and professional, and it was delivered when the Multifloids promised it. This was practically unique in the computer industry, and it was John O'Donnell, John Ruttenberg and everyone at Multiflow who did it, working night and day to get the product out. O'Donnell, particularly, was an engine of go-go-go who drove his people hard and himself even harder, to the point that he had no home life. Josh worried about him, telling him that he was risking losing his family. But John was unstoppable, driven to get the Trace to be the product he knew it could be—and he didn't let up.

As Josh stood watching the crowd at the product introduction that night, he was overcome with pride. This was the real deal, he thought; the Multifloids were the children of Alan Perlis. They took the Zen of Building and produced something beautiful. They might not know what a profit and loss statement looked like, but when it came to building machines, they were geniuses, real systems people.

I wasn't at the product introduction in New York City, and I always regretted missing it. I was so caught up in the scientific acceptance of the technology and financing the company that I didn't understand how important the official introduction would be until it was too late. I thought it would be an event like so many I had been to, without any real content—where my job was to gaze at Josh with my best Nancy Reagan adoring look. But it was a celebration—Josh's big night—and I missed it.

The summer before the product introduction Pedro Castillo, the Ruttenberg family friend who first introduced the founders to venture capital, had hosted a dinner at the Darien Country Club. Along with Josh and me, Pedro invited Don and Barbara Eckdahl, Gene and Susan Petinelli and, as guest of honor, "Buck" Rogers, an IBM marketing luminary. I was seated next to Buck and, even though I had become pretty good at talking to people I had nothing in common with, this was impossible. I tried and Buck tried. We discussed the weather, the difficulties of air travel, the complexity of the Atlanta airport—no topic lasted very long. Finally, we gave up and Buck talked across me to Josh, and I talked to Susan Petinelli. After dinner we watched the Darien Glee Club singing show tunes. Everyone watched politely, but I kept having flashbacks to high school in Omaha, Nebraska, especially since I was wearing a shirtwaist dress similar to my high school uniform.

So I skipped the product introduction and what a mistake that was! Many of our New York friends were there: Martin Davis, Al Novikoff, and Mel Hausner from NYU; Evelyn Rudahl from the Equitable. And for weeks afterward I got reports about how wonderful it had been. The evening showcased everything that I loved about the company: my husband's accomplishments and those of all the remarkable people at Multiflow. I wished I had been standing by Josh, showing him the support I felt with all my being.

Driving home from the product introduction, Josh was so hyped up from excitement that he got a speeding ticket for going seventy miles an hour in a forty mile zone on a residential street in Woodbridge in the middle of the night. One of the beautiful bouquets from the product introduction sat next to him on the car seat as he drove too fast, but it and he arrived home safely. The bouquet stayed on our dining room table for a long time, reminding us of the triumphal event.

* * *

At the Supercomputer conference in Santa Clara, CA, the following June, Multiflow introduced the Trace to industry and the scientific community—the world that had been skeptical of VLIW technology for years. There had been a constant drumbeat from the moment Josh invented VLIW, repeating that it wouldn't work. His computer science colleagues thought that it was only his selling skills that made the technology seem workable, enabling Multiflow to get as far as it had. They seemed to be saying that it was all flim-flam, that as few people could work VLIW technology as could skillfully work the Veg-O-Matic machine if they bought it and took it home.

Now with the working Trace in front of them—running the UNIX operating system, behaving like a real computer—no one could be skeptical any longer. Everyone could see that the VLIW computer performed the way Josh had been telling them for years that it would, that the technology was as good as he claimed. With programs running, potential customers could see that compiling programs before they ran did not take forever, the FUD—fear, uncertainty, and doubt—that the competition had been throwing at them. When Multiflow delivered its first product, the drumbeat saying that VLIW wouldn't work was stilled forever.

When Josh called me from Santa Clara to tell me that his technology had been vindicated, I was thrilled. I remembered the hard years at Yale after Josh introduced VLIW at ISCA in Stockholm. It seemed then that no one would accept it. Josh had felt lonely then and I felt it with him. Now everyone could see the substance I had always seen. I felt glad and very proud of him.

Multiflow shipped a machine to Santa Clara, and everyone took turns manning the booth. Booth duty was grueling, but Josh relished it. It was like giving talks, interacting with people who wanted to know about VLIW, who would be using his technology. He enjoyed the selling, especially here in Santa Clara with so many numerical analysts and questions of a higher order. And he liked showing off what the Multifloids' hard work had produced.

Josh doing booth duty

At the Multiflow booth, everyone was open and welcoming. They let people crawl all over the machine, inside as well as outside, letting them run their own programs to see how they performed. The Cydrome booth, a competitor across the conference hall floor, was different, though, and the Multifloids pointed it out to anyone who would listen. They were getting almost as good press as Multiflow, but their people kept everyone away from their machine. No one was allowed to touch it.

Cydrome used a VLIW-style architecture, the only mini-supercomputer maker with an approach similar to Multiflow. Bob Rau, the founder, was a scientist who had done important work in the same field as Josh, but because he didn't see the technology's applicability as broadly as Josh, their product was an attached processor, not a stand-alone computer.

Cydrome promised hardware far more complicated than the Trace, and the Multifloids believed that the design was too ambitious, that Bob underestimated the difficulty of engineering. Any complexity in the hardware increases the chances that something can go wrong, and everywhere the Trace was simple, the Cydrome machine was complicated. The Trace had a clean design; all the choices were conservative. The designers were striving for "plain vanilla."

Cydrome never got its computer running well and Josh thought it was unfinished at the Supercomputer Conference. He and his colleagues jeered that Cydrome was exhibiting an empty box, like the false front on a saloon in a western movie. Eventually the company went out of business, never having sold a single machine.

* * *

There were a lot of good industry analysts; Hambrecht & Quist and the Gartner Group were two of the best. They provided independent company reviews, helpful to computer industry executives, to customers and also to investors, particularly second-round and later investors who didn't want to do their own research. Like all the best analysts, they charged hefty fees for subscriptions but didn't take additional money from the companies they reported on. Stacks of their reports rested next to the Trace at the New York product introduction.

But there were many other analysts, more suspect in Josh's thinking, who produced inexpensive, widely circulated newsletters. Companies hired them to evaluate their operations, expecting coverage in the newsletter; this was the way these analysts made money. If a company didn't hire an analyst, the newsletter was written from the point of view of the competitors who did hire him. And because they were widely circulated and taken seriously, any company that didn't hire an analyst would be faced with customers or investors waving the newsletter, wanting to know about anything unfavorable in the report. Josh thought this was blackmail and resented it, but he saw it was necessary to do business.

The analysts all used industry benchmarks in their reports; the most important of these was LINPACK, a set of computer routines used to solve systems of simultaneous equations, problems found at the core of most scientific computing. Because these computations were so central, the program provided a good indication of performance on real applications. The ratio of product cost per unit of LINPACK performance, the price/performance ratio, was the most important result. All the companies competing in the mini-supercomputer market used LINPACK to measure speed; they and all the customers watched the results carefully.

Multiflow technology had always scored high on LINPACK, from the very beginning. It was early LINPACK performance, when Multiflow was designing trial machines—before the Trace, before the first financing—that got the venture capitalists' attention. John O'Donnell's insistence that a meeting be interrupted with a stellar result was a high point of the dark days after the Apollo deal died; this was the message slip that Josh still kept on his desk.

And when they had a real Trace, right after it was first assembled on the manufacturing floor, LINPACK was one of the first programs they ran on it. The Trace performance was twenty times the Pyramid performance, just like that, right out of the box. The difference was so stark that at first they thought they had done something wrong. But they hadn't; they had done something right. It was a real high-five moment.

Jack Dongarra, a numerical analyst at the Argonne National Laboratory, developed and maintained LINPACK. Since he was a reputable academic, he was a little embarrassed to be popularly known for keeping a list, but he took his responsibility seriously. When he saw how consistently Multiflow had the best price/performance ratio in the mini-supercomputer field, he became suspicious. He decided to visit Branford to see for himself.

When Multiflow ran LINPACK, they used special compiler settings which produced the best results, "teaching to the test." This was Application Support Specialist Chani Pangali's idea and he said all the companies did that—showing the straight-ahead Multiflow engineers how to be street smart in the cutthroat world of computer marketing. He called it "the honest way of cheating on LINPACK." And he was right; Josh and John looked around and all their competitors did do it—special settings for LINPACK.

Since the simultaneous equations used for the special settings were so central to scientific computing, they didn't distort the results; that wasn't what Jack was worried about. He was afraid that Multiflow was actually making up their results, really fudging; he had a hard time believing the results could be as good as they were.

When Jack did his site visit, Josh showed him the code that came out of the compiler. He could see how dense it was and how much parallelism the compiler found. Seeing the code, Jack had to believe the results were accurate. It was right in front of him. He left Branford mollified, but he continued to be uneasy and to watch Multiflow's results carefully, still worried that the numbers were too good to be true. He thought there might be something he didn't understand, some way of cheating that he hadn't figured out. He never found it, though, because Multiflow wasn't cheating. Their LINPACK numbers were really that good.

* * *

The press loved Multiflow, even before the product introduction. At first it was the local press, like the *New Haven Business Digest*, but soon it spread to the technical press and the national media.

Multiflow was lucky to have Brian Cohen and his company, Technology Solutions Inc., in charge of public relations. They found him at an early stage of his career, recommended by one of the venture capitalists. He was a

One of Brian's innovative ads

remarkable person, smart and visionary, a big thinker, as good in his field as the Multiflow scientists were in theirs. Brian's passion for Multiflow matched the founders' own. He threw himself and his tremendous intelligence into the company, mastering the subtlety of VLIW, and the company benefited. The technology so captivated him that he named his newborn son Trace Cohen—a child named after a computer.

Thanks to Brian, articles about Multiflow were everywhere, especially in the technical press. They were inescapable. *Electronic Business, Microbytes, Electrical Engineering Times, Computer World, Datamation*: the list went on and on. Josh was always meeting with someone—in his office, in their offices, across the country, always working to promote Multiflow. Josh did learn, however, that when a photographer wanted him to pose sitting cross-legged on top of a computer like a genie, he needed to refuse. He looked as silly as Michael Dukakis did in the

Josh looking silly on top of a Trace

161

1988 presidential election picture of him popping out of a tank.

The company narrative captured the press: Josh's inventing the technology, the three guys and a car, three academics finding a seasoned industry veteran and starting a company in the former SNET garage. That really got them—they loved the garage. It was a story common on the West Coast—in Palo Alto, California, in Silicon Valley where Hewlett-Packard, Apple and other companies were started in the founders' garages. But it wasn't as common in the East.

Many East Coast Chambers of Commerce were promoting their areas as new Silicon Valleys, coming up with names like Silicon Alley, the 128 Technology Corridor and Research Triangle, competing for jobs and industry with the West Coast. The Multiflow story fed this and the press jumped on it, pumping up the company's publicity. An East Coast example of entrepreneurial innovation coming out of a university—the press couldn't get enough of it.

The blurb to the left of Josh's head refers to the garage

After a while coverage spread beyond the local outlets, and we started seeing articles in the national press: *Venture,* among others, and feeds from the technical press being picked up by the Associated Press. In March and September, 1986, *Business Week* had box articles about Multiflow as a company to watch and then on April 20, 1987, right before the product introduction, there was a full page article *"WILL MULTIFLOW SET A NEW STANDARD?"* with a picture of Don and Josh by a Trace.

This Business Week article was a full page

Business Week—a full page, with a picture! Real celebration at Multiflow! Everyone read *Business Week*—investors, customers, scientists—everyone. This was the most impressive press coverage yet. Multiflow got hundreds of reprints to hand out at the product introduction, some for the information packages and some left in stacks next to the Trace for people to pick up; it was hard for anyone to leave the event without at least one reprint.

After the product introduction, Multiflow had real buzz, a mystique that took on a life of its own. It was the company to watch, the one with the compelling narrative. Press coverage continued at a relentless pace. Josh's picture was in the local press so many times, he was recognized on the street. Suddenly, he was an important person. It was a little daunting.

Our son Dave, then aged nine, became interested in computers and it was very strange for him to see his father everywhere in the press. He was proud, but he didn't quite know what to make of it. Like Josh, he was interested in technology, not the business side, which was what the articles were all about. When we brought Dave to computer camp the summer after the product introduction, I was startled to see one of these articles prominently posted— with a picture of the three Multiflow founders. Because I didn't want Dave singled out and embarrassed, I took the counselor aside and asked him to take the article down, but the publicity was inescapable.

In October, 1987, Josh was named Connecticut's Eli Whitney Entrepreneur of the Year. The award was given to the "Connecticut entrepreneur who best represented the creative legacy of Eli Whitney," whose work and life were based in New Haven. The award—one of Whitney's machine tool molds, refinished and polished to a lustrous sheen, fitted with a plaque—was sponsored by the business community including some of the Multiflow investors. Since Whitney was an engineer, Josh's winning made some sense.

But to win he beat Fred DeLuca, who started the Subway chain of sandwich stores, and even then we knew that it was all wrong. Fred was a real entrepreneur, far more than Josh, who had accidentally stumbled into it. He had built his organization on his own, using $1,000 of borrowed money—in the Horatio Alger way. Multiflow had barely begun selling machines in 1987 and the Subway chain was already showing signs of going national. I felt awkward around DeLuca at the presentation; we both did and Josh had to give a speech.

As we left the award ceremony, Josh and I shook our heads. A computer company was such a lottery ticket—a small chance at a big win. Computers were glamorous, but sandwiches were where the real entrepreneurs went—the guys who worked by themselves and conquered the world against the odds. A sandwich chain was a far better bet than a computer company for lasting into the next decade. But Connecticut wanted to be the birthplace of a computer

Josh (center) with the two Whitney award runners up, Fred DeLuca on the left. On the right is Murray Lender, founder of Lender's Bagels, who presented the award

company, not a sandwich chain.

By the end of 1987, Multiflow had shipped nineteen Trace computers, selling to Proctor & Gamble, the US Naval Weapons Research Center, Hewlett-Packard, Motorola and several universities, as well as to the beta sites. The Supercomputer Research Center—the beta site— bought a Trace 28/200, the biggest one, and paid for it before the product introduction. When payment for that first machine arrived in the Multiflow bank account, Josh took $125, as many dollars as they had employees, and passed them out at a company meeting.

"Everyone contributed to this success," said Josh. "I want each of you to have the first dollar Multiflow ever earned."

"How can we each have the first dollar?" someone asked.

"Parallel processing," Josh answered—inevitably.

NO VECTORS

It was always hard to describe Multiflow's technology and why it made the Trace go so fast. Investors never even wanted Josh to try—despite his eloquence. They said that technology talks put people to sleep, made their eyes glaze over. But Multiflow was a technology-driven company, and Josh didn't think he could just say, "It goes faster, but it would take you a lifetime to understand why." He tried so many different ways of describing the technology it made his head spin.

The confusion was very discouraging, especially since it left the investors with so many unanswered questions.

"How much faster is the Trace? And faster than what?" the investors would ask.

The answers they got from the Multifloids drove them crazy.

"You guys are like college professors—stop it, already," they said. "Just give us a number."

But there was no number. You couldn't just say that it was four times faster than a Digital Equipment VAX, because sometimes it was and sometimes it wasn't. A lot depended on what program you were running.

The real answer was something like, "for many things you want to do, the programs will get to the result far faster using the Trace than using any other computer near its cost." But that didn't have much of a marketing ring.

For anything even slightly understandable, Josh was stuck with car analogies—"your mileage may vary." And after a while investors, Don, all the Multifloids—even Leigh—got sick of car analogies and told Josh he had to stop.

This pained Josh—not being able to describe the technology and its advantages in plain English. Salesman that he was, he knew that what stuck in the customer's mind was important. Words matter, names matter—the way you describe something influences how you think about it.

Multiflow chose the machine name, the Trace, very carefully to evoke the technology. And Josh had named trace scheduling, instruction level parallelism, and VLIW to be as understandable as he could, although VLIW was not his first choice name for the technology. He tried SPIE first, Static Parallel Instruction Execution, a perfect choice since static means "done before the code runs," and the initials made a word you could say. But SPIE was already used by the world of optics and photonics so he turned to the more unwieldy VLIW. He figured that if VLSI—a popular hardware technology with a name you couldn't pronounce—could catch on, maybe he had a chance with VLIW for an architecture style. As good as the technology was and as beautifully engineered as the Trace was, if the customer was confused, he wouldn't buy it.

Josh's antenna went on alert about Trace model names during a visit to one of their beta sites. He heard customers talking about 1-wides, 2-wides and 4-wides, names denoting the number of boards in each computer. He realized they were only thinking about boards—hardware—missing the point of the technology. They didn't understand that the Trace 1-wide was doing seven operations at the same time.

He never wanted anyone thinking about boards; he wanted the number of parallel instructions firmly in the customer's mind. Josh pushed a numbering system with 7, 14 and 28 in the name, the number of parallel operations. And when they introduced the Trace, it came in three models, the 7/200, 14/200 and 28/200, with 200 referring to the series.

This hardware/software confusion was a constant fight. Investors and customers couldn't grasp that the advantage came from the software, not the hardware—the same problem Josh had at Yale when he first invented VLIW technology. People could see and touch hardware but software remained abstract. During one of the later financings, Josh sat with a particularly naïve investor, showing slides, explaining where the speed-up came from. It looked as though he was really getting it, but then the investor pointed to the picture of the computer and asked where the compiler was, not realizing it was software.

When Josh told me this story, he laughed but, really, he was discouraged. At Yale he had the frustration of computer scientists who wouldn't understand his innovation; now he had to contend with bankers. And simplify his language to the point where he thought all his meaning was lost. And I sympathized with him. His last years at Yale had been gut-wrenching; I wanted Josh to have an easier time now than he was having.

To help visitors at Multiflow understand the technology, Josh always tried to take them into Stefan Freudenberger's office to see his DAG—short for "directed acyclic graph." This was a large computer print-out of the compiler tracing its way through the code, a visual depiction of the way it found parallelism. Stefan had hand colored it to illustrate the functions of the paths; it was beautiful—an art-work worthy of a museum.

Stefan's DAG was color coded, with each color indicating a different aspect of the code

But Josh never could get visitors into Stefan's office, despite his telling them that the DAG showed what was really going on. Instead they wanted to see the factory floor, sure that was where the magic happened. So Josh shook his head, by-passed Stefan's office, and took his visitors to see the assembly floor, even though it was minimal. All the Multifloids did there was to put together the boards that had been manufactured elsewhere. But it was the most popular spot on the tour.

To fight the confusion—to get the software's advantage into people's heads—everyone at Multiflow tried to think up catchy slogans. But it seemed impossible. The trick was to be simple, understandable, and correct, but it seemed as though you could get any two of those, never all three.

Brian Cohen, the publicist, couldn't describe the technology, but he was good at slogans, far better than any of the Multifloids. He was a master of making the vagueness catchy—not precise; no slogan could make the vagueness precise, but catchy. In his words Multifloids were "the architects of high speed computing." Everyone liked that. But it didn't solve the problem of making the technology understandable.

Early in Multiflow's history Leigh and Bob Nix took a crack at trying to find a slogan to describe the technology advantage. They wanted a premium to give to employees, investors and friends—and to customers, later on. And the give-away needed a slogan on it, something pithy to remind people of the company. Leigh asked Bob for ideas and for a while they had fun playing around.

The most successful of the Trace's competitors were vector machines which performed extremely regular computations on data in rows, called vectors. Leigh and Bob wanted to take a swipe at these machines which, unlike the Trace, required laborious hand coding to work well. Gleefully, they produced coffee mugs and buttons with a red circle and slash through the word "vectors." No Vectors.

These party favors were a big hit—everyone loved them. The Multifloids all wore the buttons at work. Investors and customers all got mugs. I had a "No Vectors" button and wore it to class and the grocery store, getting very strange looks in the process—people asked me if I was making some sort of political statement. I didn't care, though; I loved my button and wore it proudly.

At the Santa Clara product introduction, computer scientists and engineers snapped up the buttons— particularly numerical analysts whose profession was based on vectors. Grinning, button-wearing scientists were everywhere; you couldn't walk on the conference floor without seeing them.

But the slogan backfired. Again, the subtlety of the technology caused problems. The Trace was actually best on code with lots of vectors. Companies that used vectors were the target customers. So "No Vectors" was the wrong message to send; you didn't want your customers thinking you couldn't handle what they specialized in.

Like so much about VLIW technology, "No Vectors" was shorthand for a complicated message. It really meant that to run code on the Trace, the programmer didn't need to *identify* vectors. On vector machines the programmer had to pay attention to the code structure for the computer to take advantage of the vectors; the Trace, in contrast, did that all by itself. It did the job differently but got the same results without the extra work. And the Trace could make the non-vector part of the code go fast, too, unlike vector machines.

They could have said "No Vector Machines" or " No Vectorizing," or "We're better on Vectors—Please buy our Computer."

Or as Bob Colwell said, "You feed me any junky spaghetti-like code and I will run my magical compiler on it and extract all that wonderful parallel performance. Then, it will run lickety-split and you will be so happy. But we're good at vector codes just like vector machines."

But that wouldn't be as catchy. Catchy phrases and VLIW technology didn't mix well.

Eventually Multiflow selected a logo and no one used "No Vectors" any more. This went a long way toward professional presentation; it was stylish, if not explanatory. Eric Bovell, the mechanical engineer that John O'Donnell hired away from Prime Computer, knew a design house that specialized in logos. Since this company had designed the outside of the Trace, a plain refrigerator-style box, it understood Multiflow's style. The competition's computer boxes sported an endless array of blinking lights across fancy anodized black aluminum and brushed stainless steel boxes, but Multiflow never wanted glitzy. It wanted a distinctive logo, something elegant but nothing space-aged. Radical technology in a conservative guise.

When the design house was ready to show the logo designs, a big group of Multifloids assembled: Josh and Don, John and John, the marketing team, Leigh and a few of the engineers. But to their surprise, everything the logo house showed them seemed boring and pedestrian.

Conservative design didn't have to be boring. What happened to elegant? The Multiflow team just sat there.

"Isn't there anything else?" asked Josh.

Maybe they planned it this way or maybe the designs they brought out next really were rejects, but the rest of the designs were different. They were logos that an individual designer had liked but the whole team hadn't agreed on. These were the innovative ones.

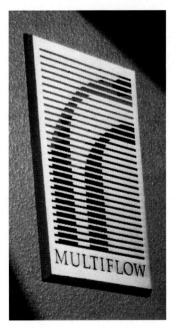

And one was perfect. It was the start of an "M," a sweep of bars, graceful, with artistic imperfections.

"Wait a minute—that's not quite right," said someone in the room.

"Yes, exactly," said Josh. He thought the irregular lines and black shapes evoked the long instruction words.

And it became their logo.

* * *

When Multiflow started in 1984, Josh's presentation graphics were minimal, the slides typewritten and photocopied onto acetate transparencies. This was the way all academics did it in those days; fancy graphics were limited to large corporations.

When Don arrived, he wanted Multiflow to upgrade to professional graphics and Josh thought that sounded good. He was always looking for more effective ways to explain the technology. He just wasn't sure how to go about getting a more professional look.

Don suggested that Josh use a production house for his slides. He pictured Josh explaining what he wanted to the technicians who would figure out what the slides should look like. They would use one of the fancy graphics packages available then and produce typeset slides with figures and graphs.

Josh gave it a try, although he was dubious—he was far too much of a perfectionist to give someone else control of how he presented the technology. He went to a production house that did graphics for T Rowe Price since their venture arm, Alex Brown was a Multiflow investor. Maybe this would make them more technically sophisticated than the other production houses. But the graphic designers couldn't understand what Josh was trying to say—the *audience* could barely understand it, how much harder must it have been for the nontechnical designers? Gibberish resulted—strings of technical terms grouped in random order; it was a real waste of time and money. Josh ended up redoing the whole thing himself.

But Josh was also a showman and he agreed with Don that they needed professional graphics to get his points across better. So he set out to find a way to do it himself and asked people at the production house what software package they used. "Mirage" was their answer. Then he asked someone else, who also turned out to use Mirage. Without making any decisions, he called Mirage and told them he was buying their software and asked what printer worked best with the software.

It was hard to get an answer, since Mirage needed to work with all the printers—and didn't want to alienate anybody. Finally, after swearing Josh to secrecy, the guy he talked to recommended a Calcomp thermal plotter—a Colormaster—which transfers color directly from film, resulting in vivid colors.

Then Josh called Calcomp.

"Hey guys, we're getting one of your plotters. Can you tell me, are there any software packages that are particularly good, that work best with your printer?"

Again, it was hard to get an answer. They didn't want to favor any of their applications, either. Finally:

"Well, you didn't hear it from us; we have to work with all the packages. But, Mirage—that's great stuff."

"Okay—sounds good," Josh said. It sounded like the right marriage.

Multiflow bought Mirage and a Calcomp Colormaster and Josh brought them home, installing them in the mudroom alcove off our breakfast room. He worked hard every night after dinner, mastering the tricky graphics package. He knew computers, but the artistic mechanics were all new to him.

The results were beautiful. After a while Josh was getting exactly what he wanted, printed in wonderful colors. He could see that his audiences responded far better to these slides than to his typewritten ones. They still had trouble with the subtlety of the technology—but at least now they were paying attention.

For most of his presentations Josh used slides on acetate transparencies printed by the Colormaster. They were easy to transport and, wherever he went, he knew he could count on using an overhead projector. But Mirage also provided solid and sweep backgrounds for 35mm slides and Josh produced some of those, too, using a production house in New York.

After a while Multifloids noticed how professional Josh's presentations looked. At first it was only a buzz, but then John and John asked for copies of the slides. Then they wanted slides of their own design. Then other people wanted copies of Josh's slides or ones of their own. Soon Josh was producing slides all the time, supplying the whole company.

It was too much. It was too much right away, but after the product introduction, demand for Josh's slides exploded. He couldn't keep up with the demand. It was taking time from his real work; he couldn't keep on doing this. At his wits end, Josh suggested that I learn Mirage and produce slides as a contractor for Multiflow. This would take the burden off him and provide Multiflow with a reliable source of high-quality graphics. Even though I am not a computer scientist, he trusted me to pay attention to the nuances and to work until I got it right. The company would have slides, and Josh could still create his own presentations.

Between college and working at the Equitable, I had trained as an artist, thinking that I would spend my life painting. I had stopped, though, when it didn't go anywhere, and it had been years since I had drawn. Presentation graphics was different, but it was enough the same as drawing that I thought it would be familiar. And I thought that this was something I might like.

I was working on my MBA at night then and home with the kids and studying during the day. I had taken two or three classes a term at first but, as Multiflow got more exciting, my interest waned and I slowed to one class at a time. Presentation graphics seemed like something I could do, even though I had never used software more complicated than word processing. And with the kids in elementary school, I had plenty of time to take on a new project.

When Multiflow started I had worked for the founders, finding office space and employee benefits. The company had been small then, and my work had started to feel claustrophobic, as though I were working for my husband, so I stopped as soon as it was practical. Now, though, Multiflow was big enough that I thought I could work there as an independent contractor. And it was so exciting, I longed to take a more active part .

It took me some time to master Mirage, since it was a complicated program. But once I got back into drawing, I loved it. I added a digitizer—a tablet used with a stylus—to the equipment for more freeform drawing capacity; Josh

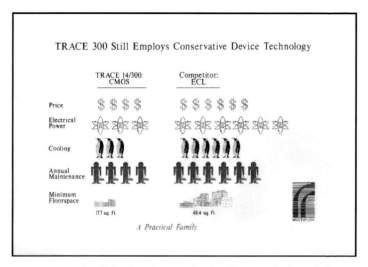

**My penguin slide, flamboyant for its day, used a lot of the
meager Mirage clip-art**

had only been using a mouse. Most of the slides I did were
word slides, but every so often, I got to draw. It was a
wonderfully artistic, creative process and a lot of fun—
drawing to tell a story. And I made liberal use of the
limited clip-art that came with Mirage.

To avoid conflicts of interest, my business—Creative
Visuals—contracted with the Multiflow marketing
department. Josh stayed as far away as he could from
ordering work or paying me. And he continued to make
most of his own slides, using the Multiflow Colormaster
when it was free.

It worked well—keeping us separate, but sometimes I
got confused. I had two roles with Multiflow now:
contractor producing graphics and founder's wife with a
Nancy Reagan smile. And there were times when I couldn't
make up my mind who I was, for instance, when a
Marketing Assistant sent me flowers after I did a rush job
for her on short notice. I simply didn't know what to do. I

was embarrassed—but I liked being appreciated. Mostly, though, I was too busy to worry about it.

When I began producing slides, I thought I would be working only a few days a week, but I had underestimated demand. Once there was a reliable way to get good graphics without bothering Josh, demand exploded even more than it had after the product introduction. The scientists who gave talks wanted them; the salespeople wanted them. And once there were new slides available, from any source, all the sales people wanted those, too, in acetate transparencies and 35mm. I would get rush jobs to produce thirty sets of thirty slides, then another set. Then another set. The Colormaster was going all the time—and it was a tricky machine. I learned its quirks the way some teenaged boys learned about cars, developing a real affection for it, a feel for what it needed, taking it apart and putting it back together. I ordered boxes of thermal film from California and extra parts—the racks to mount the thermal film—because it was always jamming.

When Josh was away for a few days, as he often was during the week, I set up jobs to go all night—the same way Bob Colwell did when he was designing the CPU. At night I could listen to the printer from my bedroom while I slept, and when the printer ran out of film or when it jammed, I woke up. Just like when I was breast-feeding my children, the noise—the lack of noise, in this case—woke me. I could tend to the printer without really waking up, just as I had with breast-feeding, and then go back to bed. And then I would sleep on until the printer called me again. This went on week after week, month after month, since I had so many big print jobs to do. I slept while the Colormaster worked but the vigilance took its toll. I was constantly busy, constantly tired and glad, then, that I was only taking one MBA class at a time.

To produce 35mm slides from Mirage files, I uploaded data to a production house in New York which would then FedEx the completed slides back to me. It was a small company, run by a few observant Jews who closed down during the Sabbath. The owner told me that he spent the time from sundown Friday until sundown Saturday with his family, not thinking about work, as required by Jewish law. He said that the answering machine would be on and that he would get back to me as soon as he could.

When I heard this, I was bemused. It sounded heavenly and I imagined my life that way: not thinking about work, with an untended answering machine on for a whole day.

I was so tired then and so was Josh. The idea of twenty-four hours every single week where neither Josh nor I could think about Multiflow, really closing ourselves off with the kids, was an impossible dream since our lives had taken on a frenzy that never let up. I loved the idea of a full day of rest, even though I knew I could never sell it to Josh. He could never pause like that. He was too involved with making Multiflow a success to stop working for even twenty-four hours each week.

LE FLIC

"Does Dorothy's daddy work on an airplane?" our daughter's friends asked. And sometimes it seemed that way.

"Is he in sales?" This from a friend of mine about my scientist husband. But when I described Josh's work and she said "at that level, they're all in sales," I realized she was right.

When Josh and I were first married, we wondered if either of us might someday travel regularly for business. Josh's Aunt Anne traveled selling shower curtains and wall paper for her design firm and, even though she went to places like Indianapolis, we still thought it sounded great—a lot of fun, with someone else to pay for it.

At Multiflow the travel fantasy came true. But as they say, "be careful what you wish for."

Josh's work promoting Multiflow to finance the company transitioned seamlessly into customer support, and he was always on an airplane. Anytime, anywhere they needed the big guns, Josh had to go. Prospects and customers continued to want him talking up the technology. And he went to distributors of applications software, too, to convince them to include the Trace in their next application release because if customers couldn't run their programs, they wouldn't buy a computer. And there was always the press to visit and investors—always investors.

Sometimes the travel was glamorous or adventurous, like our youthful fantasies, and then I was jealous, wishing I was with him. The VCs held receptions in Bath, England and the Monterey Bay Aquarium, closing them down for glorious private parties. And once Josh rode in the seat next to Jane Pauley on a red-eye coming back from San Francisco; since I was a *Today* show fan, I was green with envy. Josh said the flight attendants were clearly used to her being there, and she used her own pillow, mask, and blanket to turn her seat by the window into a bed, saying only "good-night" before she turned over and went to sleep for the entire flight. And another time Josh was on a twenty-four person puddle jumper late at night, going from Toronto to Buffalo, NY, the only other passenger besides the rock group U-2. Josh found the group ordinary—tired, irritable-seeming Brits throwing insults at each other, nothing to get excited about, but I was impressed when he told me about it.

The only time Josh admitted he was star-struck was when he rode home from Brussels with three members of the Modern Jazz Quartet. He had been behind them on the check-in line at TWA, watching the affectionate, tearful parting of the MJQ members and their admirers who were staying in Europe. It was quite a show.

The road manager checked in instrument after instrument, rolling them out one after another like clowns getting out of a clown car as the desk agent got more and more alarmed.

"You didn't tell us that you were bringing an orchestra!" she cried out finally, in frustration.

"But Madame," the road manager replied, "we are merely a quartet."

On the plane Josh was seated very close to them, since he had been upgraded to Business Class. And the ride was suddenly more fun with the MJQ there, Milt Jackson charming the three kids on board. Josh got to tell Connie Kay how much he liked his backing of a jazz singer on an album he had been listening to recently—a real thrill.

It was almost as glamorous, but not as much fun, when Multiflow sold a Trace to the University of Catania in Sicily: Josh addressed a subcommittee of the Italian Parliament in Rome. Before getting into the parliament building, he was patted down; then he went through a medieval corridor to a glass door leading to a tiny room with six-inch-thick glass walls. While he stood in that room, seven heavily armed, uniformed men stared at him with electronic machines going in the background. Josh was taken aback by the level of security, never having seen automatic weapons guarding anything in the US. It reminded him of Adolph Eichmann's trial in 1962, where Eichmann was confined to a glass booth to prevent his assassination: scary, like nothing in the US at that time.

After he passed scrutiny in the glass cubical, Josh was led into a conference room paneled in dark mahogany. He sat at a large table with Members of the Italian Parliament, professors, industry people and their aides. After five hours, bored by discussions in Italian he didn't understand, Josh got up on cue and gave a short speech saying how honored Multiflow was to place a machine at an institution as prestigious as the University of Catania. Then the sale was approved and Josh left.

That Trace stayed in Catania for many years, in constant use, predisposing the University to the VLIW philosophy for decades. Jack Schwartz at NYU had a student in Catania, Alfredo Ferro, who told Josh many times how thrilled he was to work on the Trace, a machine with technology whose inventor he actually knew.

Josh traveled so much that the world became his office. He had favorite hotels in the cities he went to frequently, and if he had to be anywhere more than two nights, he completely unpacked, filling the hotel dressers and closets. It was more homey that way, less depressing, and he could sleep better, though he never slept well on the road. And when he ran into flight crews behaving like ugly Americans in foreign countries—loudly in a London wine bar, for instance—he felt more charitable toward them than he would have years before, knowing it was their office, too, and that they had a very hard job.

He got used to being in foreign countries and became comfortable in new cultures, picking up foreign phrases quickly with his cosmopolitan ability to adapt to new circumstances. When he traveled to Germany with Stefan Freudenberger, the German compiler engineer, he picked up so many phrases that by the end of the day, Stefan was furious with Josh for not having told him he spoke German.

Years earlier, during Josh's first year at Yale, he bought a record, "The Sound of Kinshasa," at the Yale Co-op and discovered African Music of the 1950s and 60s. In 1987, when Paul Simon released *Graceland*, he listened to it over and over, even though his real music interest lay north of South Africa. It was the wild, swooping rhythm, the complicated harmonies of Franco and the rest of the Kinshasa Sound and ET Mensa's Highlife music from Ghana that grabbed him.

Josh discovered that he could find this music, so rare in the US, in the African neighborhoods of European capitals. When I traveled with him, as I sometimes did, we always went to African street fairs, in Paris, Rome, London or

Lisbon. You could count on finding stands of cassettes—and some of them would be perfect. Then he discovered Stern's African Record Centre in Piccadilly, London. Whenever he was there, he always stopped in. And he sent lists of music he wanted with any Multifloid going to London, usually Bob Smith, the VP of Sales and Marketing, ending up at the African Record Centre, a new experience for this Texan.

Josh traveled alone or with colleagues and sometimes with the computer salesmen, who had never known what to think of him. In the evenings on those trips there were often poker games and Josh usually won, his uncle Harry having taught him strategies for playing against mediocre players. The salesmen didn't mind; in fact, they were reassured when Josh won. They didn't understand him, and they thought his winning meant that they were staking their future on a winner.

Josh became an expert on air travel and several times got the crew to open the airplane door when he arrived at the gate after it had been closed for the flight. And once, when Pilgrim Airways canceled a flight, he got them to reroute the next flight directly to New Haven instead of stopping in New London first. This happened by accident; when he started talking to the people at Pilgrim Air, he didn't actually think he could get them to change an established flight plan. He had just been bored during the enforced four hour delay and amused himself by working his way up the chain of command until he got to someone who could make a decision.

"Look in your computer—you'll see," he said. "Most of your passengers are going to New Haven. You have delayed all these people."

The agent said he would see what he could do and when the announcement came that the next plane would go directly to New Haven, the waiting area erupted with cheers. And he got home earlier than he had feared.

On one trip after a red-eye from California, Josh was met at the airport by a car carrying a recruit for him to interview. This wasn't unusual; since he had so many demands on his time, the staff tried to maximize it, booking every instant. But he was expecting Chani Pangali, the applications support specialist. He got in the car and was disoriented to find, instead, a very pale Englishman, Chris Chaney, the prospective European sales manager. Confused, Josh realized he had no idea what he was supposed to be doing.

"Yeah, yeah, you can meet with Chaney, ride back from the airport with him," Bob Smith had said.

And Josh heard "Chani."

But he recovered and interviewed Chaney, having become used to strange places and just having to get on with his job.

He traveled so much he needed new pages sewn into his passport, the entrance and exit stamps running over the allowed space. He was so tired that he sometimes became disoriented in elevators, having to look at the buttons to remember which continent he was on, the zero for the first floor telling him he was in Europe.

I itched to go along on a lot of these trips and sometimes I did—to California or Europe—places I had always wanted to go. These were fun; I loved being with Josh in new places, but I began to understand why he was complaining about how hard the traveling life was. I started noticing people in airline clubs having conversations with their kids in the evenings, trying to conduct their family life from far away. It really brought home to me how hard it was on Josh when he was the parent calling from the airline club. The parents I saw seemed so sad as they went over homework, talked about their children's problems or told them they loved them. Josh came home every weekend, except when he was in the Far East, so that when the kids needed him, he was always there. But often it was on the phone. This was a real downside of travel, one Josh had been telling me about.

Travel was physically exhausting with rigid schedules, time changes, long hours and the constant pressure to do more with every single minute. There were delays, discomfort, boredom, and a lot of indignities.

"Oh, the glamour of business travel," Josh would say, sarcastically, and I could understand his bitterness.

When he talked to John Ruttenberg about it, John described his ideal business trip—the one he could get out of going on. And this became the fantasy, the "John

Ruttenberg upgrade"—not going at all—and it looked better and better.

"You get a card!" John said, describing his dream. "You flash it at anyone who wants you to travel. You get to stay home!" It never happened enough for Josh.

I worried about his health, about the kind of toll the exhaustion, lack of exercise, and poor eating were taking on his body. I wanted Multiflow's success, but I saw how out of shape and overweight Josh was becoming, and I thought about all the stress-related diseases driven executives were prone to. A heart attack didn't seem impossible.

After a while, Josh could nap anywhere and it was a good thing since he slept so poorly on the road. In 1985, he was going to California with O'Donnell, Nix and Lowney when their plane was delayed for two hours at JFK. Josh was so exhausted that he found a good patch of carpet—all the chairs were taken in the mob scene—and lay down in his business suit, using his briefcase for a pillow, sleeping soundly for ninety minutes. The other Multifloids thought he was insane, but he had no choice; he was that exhausted.

When he was able, he stayed an extra day in new countries to see the foreign cities he visited—and sometimes he brought me to share his adventure. This charmed his hosts, so used to American executives totally oblivious to their surroundings and probably helped Multiflow sales, too.

"This is Josh Fisher. He *gets* it," the Italian distributor said when he introduced him to European customers.

But the times he got to explore or travel with me were too rare. During one of the Multiflow financings, Josh went to Edinburgh to meet potential investors. He wanted to see the city, hoped he would have a little time, but it was not to be. He was met at the airport by a black and cream Daimler automobile with a tartan blanket covering the seat and driven to his meeting on Princes Street. He gave his talk, looking through a large window across the ravine at the castle, tantalizingly close. Then he got back in the car and was driven to the airport to fly off to his next meeting. And that was the way it usually was, rushing in and out of towns, missing the sights.

* * *

In February, 1987, Josh was invited to give a talk at a conference organized by INRIA, the French national research institute. He got on the plane not realizing that a few months earlier France had begun requiring visas for American citizens. Josh had been in France many times before; he had never needed a visa, so it didn't occur to him to check. TWA was supposed to look for the visa in his passport before he got on the plane, but they didn't ask to see it.

Josh got off the red-eye at 7:00 am and headed to the immigration desk, getting ready to go to the University of Paris to give his talk at 9:00 am. Before he got to the desk, though, an immigration official pulled him aside. He was checking for visas.

"Visa? I'm supposed to have a visa?"

"Pas de probleme," the official said, and sent him to another desk. No problem for them—big problem for Josh.

The official at the desk explained the new visa requirement, saying that TWA would be fined and required to take him back.

"But I was invited by an agency of the French government," Josh protested. "They never told me I needed a visa; can't anything be done?"

The official sent him to the immigration police, telling him to explain the situation to them and surrender his passport.

"Over there," pointing.

So off Josh went, on to the next stop, trying to get past immigration. He was used to complicated negotiations, used to European bureaucracy and government officials; he had never had a problem he couldn't talk his way out of. He wasn't very worried.

The immigration police officer was a tall, thin, very angry North African with an acne-scarred face, a cigarette drooping disdainfully from his lip, and a submachine gun. He looked like he had just stepped out of a Grade B French Foreign Legion movie. Josh thought of him as "Le Flic," French slang for policeman.

He surrendered his passport, but when he tried to explain about the conference and INRIA—haltingly, in his college French—Le Flic cut him off, bursting into rapid-fire French. Josh could understand some of what he said, but when he asked him to speak more slowly, Le Flic only talked faster, his body language aggressive and hostile. Josh got the idea that here was someone who wished he didn't exist. Someone with an automatic weapon. And his passport. He didn't like it at all.

Josh sat down to think. He couldn't get past immigration, but he realized that he was free to roam the part of the airport on his side of the barrier. He had plenty of French money and there were shops, restaurants, and bathrooms—everything he needed. And there was a pay phone.

It was early morning then, and Paris was just waking up. First he called the INRIA office, but it wasn't open yet. Then he called the US embassy. Maybe they could get him into France.

When he finally reached the right person at the embassy, she told him that his case was hopeless; she had been dealing with the visa problem for months. The only way they could get him in now was with documented evidence of a dying relative. He needed to get back on the airplane and return to the US.

"Oh, well, I guess I'm going home," he thought, glancing at the board to see when planes were scheduled. But first he needed to get through to INRIA and tell them he wasn't going to make it.

The office was open now, and his call got switched around a lot, but he finally got to the right person, Mlle. Chirah.

"Oh, no; pas de probleme," she said when he described the situation. She'd make a couple of phone calls, she said. She was confident there would be no problem getting Josh into the country.

"Just wait about 45 minutes and go back to the person who has your passport," she said. Easy for her to say; she hadn't seen Le Flic.

Josh wasn't happy about approaching Le Flic, but he did as instructed—and got nothing but abuse. Angry verbal abuse and an automatic weapon. Josh had never seen anything like this, thirteen years before 9/11. It scared him.

He called Mlle. Chirah at INRIA back.

"Oh, I called the right person, there should be no problem. Let me make some more phone calls. Wait and check back with the immigration police."

So he did it again, and Le Flic got angrier. He dismissed Josh, disdainfully. Still with the automatic weapon.

This happened three more times. Each time Josh called INRIA, Mlle. Chirah told him that the problem was fixed and each time Le Flic rudely berated him, even when Josh reported the name of the Mlle. Chirah's very important person who had personally authorized his getting into the country. Le Flic wasn't impressed by the name—and snarled.

By this time, it was morning in the US and Josh called me. He had been back and forth with Le Flic several times and was pretty worked up. I got pretty upset, too, sorry for all that he was going through.

When we hung up, I made breakfast and got the kids ready for school; I didn't want to burden them since there was really no news to tell. But that day, with me trying to hide my emotions, Jane Pauley on the *Today* show which I was watching during breakfast did our family no favors. There was a long segment on the civil war in Lebanon describing kidnappings, explosions, and the hijacking of a TWA jet. That war had been going on for a few years, but in January, 1987, there had been several kidnappings of westerners, including Terry Waite, the Anglican envoy, just two weeks before Josh's Paris trip. Not a good mix at breakfast when you have a loved-one overseas.

As we watched television that morning, the kids could tell I was upset. Dorrie, just five then, decided that the problem was the war in Lebanon and that somehow her father was involved. I turned off the television quickly and tried to explain.

"No, no; Daddy's in Paris—very far from Lebanon," I said. "He's fine; he just can't get into France."

But it was too late. When Josh called again, I got more agitated, terrifying Dorrie even more. Explanations were futile; she was really upset. She became more and more convinced that her father was in Lebanon in the middle of a war, in danger of being abducted.

I tried to calm myself so I wouldn't transfer any more of my worry to her, but Josh kept calling with more bad news. And I kept getting more upset. I didn't want him to stop calling—I wanted to know what was happening. But I was scaring my poor child.

When I took Dorrie to nursery school, I spoke to her teacher, telling her that there really was nothing wrong. I hoped that the normalcy of school would calm Dorrie down, that her teachers and friends would reassure her.

In Paris as well as Woodbridge it was getting later and later. Josh's talk was originally scheduled to be the first of the day, but the organizers kept pushing it back as INRIA tried to get him into the country. He was one of the few scientists with international reputations scheduled to talk at the meeting, and they really wanted him there.

"Professor Fisher is still stuck at immigration," the announcement came—in Europe, once a professor, always a professor. Each time Josh called with an update, they made another announcement, postponing for another hour. And then another hour. On into the afternoon. But the talk wasn't happening.

At the Charles De Gaulle airport, Josh looked at the departures board and was alarmed to see that the last flight to the US for the day was leaving. He tried to think what to do next; it didn't look like he would make it to the conference. He pictured sleeping on chairs at the airport all night, and that was the best case. The worst case was that French immigration might put him somewhere; he didn't want to be wherever Le Flic wanted him put—not the Georges V, that was for sure. He had given up on INRIA, having been at it for eight hours now. He thought maybe he should get his passport back from Le Flic and fly somewhere else—London for the night, for instance.

He called the American Embassy again. They hadn't been able to help him get into the country, but maybe they had a suggestion for what he should do now. He spoke to the same woman at the embassy he had spoken to that morning.

"Aha!" she said. "You are still here. Things are different now. When you called this morning, you were the one who had done something wrong, arriving without a visa. The mistake was yours. Now, with all the planes to the US gone, you have been mistreated at the hands of the French government. *That* we can complain about. And if we can complain about it, we can get you in. Wait 45 minutes and call me back."

When Josh called back, the embassy official's boss had spoken to the Inspecteur Divisionaire at the Quai d'Orsay, Le Flic's boss. In a half hour a courier would be there with instructions; Josh would be allowed into France. Just like that.

Josh called INRIA and told them to schedule his talk for 4:30 pm, the last talk of the day. It looked as though he was getting in. And a half hour after his second call to the US embassy, a short, stout, dark black-skinned man in a business suit went into Le Flic's office with a briefcase. Then they called him in.

Le Flic was hopping mad. He had lost and he didn't like it; he was shaking like a coiled spring. Josh couldn't imagine that he would really be shot, but he realized that if he was ever going to worry about it, this would be the time.

Le Flic grudgingly sold him a visa, and Josh and the courier left the office. Ten minutes later, at immigration, the admitting officer looked at the visa and did a double take—then he let him into France and the courier drove him to the University of Paris for his INRIA talk.

Josh felt as though he had emerged from a surreal world and was now back where everything made sense—away from Le Flic—in the familiar academic environment. And when he stepped up to the podium at the conference, there was thunderous applause from the attendees who had been following his progress as the talk kept being postponed, hour by hour, throughout the entire day.

When Dorrie got home from nursery school back in Woodbridge, I told her that her father was safe in France, that everything was okay. She understood what I said, but the fear didn't leave her; for years she was afraid whenever she heard about Lebanon.

And forever after, as long as Josh had that passport, whenever he entered France, border officials did a double-take when they saw that visa. Josh knew it was coming and waited for it. He presented his passport: turn page, turn page, turn page, WHOA! They would hold the passport up, look at the visa, look at Josh, look again. He asked people what kind of visa it was and never got a good answer. Someone said it was something they gave to couriers who transported prisoners, but that made no sense. People said it was a police visa but he never learned what kind. It was a mystery, a souvenir of his experience with Le Flic.

SELLING THE TRACE

Before the product introduction, an analyst at the Gartner Group told Josh that once Multiflow had customers, he wouldn't know what hit him.

"You're living this relaxed life now. You think you know how panicked you will be, but you don't. Here's how you will be living..."

Josh thought it was impossible. After all he had been through, his life couldn't get more frantic. But the analysts were right. The minute they delivered a Trace to the first beta site—the early customers—the whole world changed. Life sped up, more than anyone thought possible. It was hectic, the demands exhausting, even though the sales were thrilling.

An early Gartner report on Apollo called it an exciting company, but asked what would happen when Apollo got to the "inevitable boredom of running a company." They asked the same about Multiflow, but they were wrong—about both companies. Apollo longed for it, longed for the boredom; Multiflow longed for it, and so did Josh.

Josh took the first order for a Trace, and he or O'Donnell made at least one site visit to each of the first nineteen customers. Since Multiflow was a small new company, based on new ideas, customers wanted to hear from the founders, not just from the salespeople. Both of them were intimately involved in the selling—but more Josh than John.

Besides governments and universities, Multiflow sold computers mostly to manufacturing companies. Many fell into a market segment Josh called "death and destruction," the Trace having the advanced computing power needed to design products for the defense industry. This included aircraft: Sikorsky, Grumman, and their competitors, but the purest example was the Supercomputer Research Center, another of the Multiflow beta sites. The SRC was a division of the National Security Agency, and whenever Josh visited, he was escorted everywhere, red lights flashing, since he didn't have a security clearance.

To support these and other customers, Multiflow hired experts like Mike Frisch, a leading light in molecular modeling who worked with users in the chemical industry. Mike's joining was a real endorsement of VLIW technology since the programs he developed for chemical analysis were so compute-intensive that they stressed every machine they were run on. And they hired consultants: Jerzy Wasniewski, an expert in mathematical modeling and Wolfgang Gentzsch, a physicist expert in computational fluid dynamics, too.

This was the Multiflow pattern—John O'Donnell's idea—to get the best people with application expertise to support users. Just as he had championed Mike Loukides, who had a PhD in English from Stanford, to write the manuals, O'Donnell wanted really smart people with professional credentials in customer support.

And I continued to make slides, now supporting the sales force more than the financial people, the Colormaster going day and night as it churned out transparencies. I had far more of those restless nights when I set up jobs and slept, waiting for the machine to jam or need a new ribbon as it produced the sales materials. It was hectic, the pressure endless.

Computers were selling steadily, though not as fast as everyone hoped, and potential customers toured the plant in a constant stream. There was a company crisis when Phillip Morris executives visited, because Multiflow was a nonsmoking worksite, rare in those days. Would they send these men outside to smoke? They discussed it and discussed it, circling the question. The founders and engineers wanted to hold firm and, to their surprise and delight, Don backed them up. The Phillip Morris executives went outside to smoke when they visited Branford, despite the rain that inauspiciously fell that day. And Phillip Morris still bought a computer.

Most of the companies that bought the Trace loved it. And, usually, customers were easy to get along with because the product ran so well, so effortlessly out of the box. If there was a problem, Multiflow sent someone out to fix it, and the customer was happy since he was already getting so much more than he ever thought possible.

Motorola, though, was different. They wanted exactly what they thought they should be getting, the fastest speeds anyone suggested might be possible. If an application ran on their Trace at 27 seconds when they thought it should run at 25 seconds, Motorola wanted it fixed. They weren't impressed that another application, which they expected to run at 50 seconds, ran at 37 seconds; they wanted the top of everything. And this was hard. Just like with automobile gas mileage—"your mileage may vary"—it is hard to tell in advance how fast a program will run in real-life conditions because there are too many variables.

O'Donnell may have over-promised, not stressing how inexact his numbers were, but Motorola seemed unrealistically inflexible in their demands. Teams of people went down to the Motorola R&D lab in Phoenix trying to figure out how to make the customer happy. Again and again they went. Finally, Josh succeeded, promising better performance with compensation if the computer didn't run at a particular speed by a set date and a free upgrade to the next Trace series. He gave away a lot, but everyone at Multiflow was glad to have this difficult customer off their backs.

As challenging as they were as a customer, Motorola was worse as a supplier. They made the Trace gate arrays, the heart of the machine, and they were Multiflow's only source. After promising to continue production, Motorola abruptly stopped, leaving Multiflow to scramble for a source for their single most vital part. If O'Donnell hadn't, at the last minute, convinced National Semiconductor to manufacture their gate arrays, Multiflow would have had serious problems.

And Motorola's own products, the few workstations that Multiflow bought, never seemed to perform as well as the salespeople said they would. It was confusing. How could they be so demanding when their own product wasn't working very well? It seemed more like a vendetta than a normal business relationship. Josh wondered for a while if Motorola wanted to go into the mini-supercomputer business and was trying to discredit them, particularly when they stopped producing the gate arrays. After all this, Multiflow did as little business with Motorola as possible.

* * *

When the Trace was introduced, it didn't go as fast as it could. Rich Lethin engineered the first upgrade and he did it almost single handedly. He did it despite expectations, through hard work and perseverance, and everyone at Multiflow thanked him for it. He was a real hero.

Rich was part of the CPU development team that designed the first floating point board, the board responsible for arithmetic involving decimals or scientific notation. When he realized that the design relied on an outdated floating point chip, Rich yelled long and loud, adamant that the Trace needed the most powerful parts. He told everyone that this couldn't go on; the product was too good not to have the latest technology available.

Only one part needed changing, but to fix it they would have had to reengineer the whole board. And that would mean that the tables in the compiler would need changing—and all the code running on the customers' computers would have to be recompiled. So even though it was frustrating that programs could go faster, there was no time to worry about it. The Trace was introduced with the slower floating point chip.

Rich complained to Josh, John O'Donnell and Don—and to any engineer who would listen to him.

"Yeah, yeah, we'll get to it sometime," they said and ignored him.

But Rich wouldn't have any of this. In classic, entrepreneurial American fashion, he began to reengineer the floating point board in his off-hours. Josh and John O'Donnell knew what he was doing but looked the other way. In his assigned job he was incredibly productive, accomplishing everything he was hired to do. Management let him amuse himself, giving him unusual freedom for a low-level employee—to see what he would come up with. He was obviously a tremendously bright kid and fun to have around; they were getting their money's worth. Why not let him fool around?

And when he was done, Rich had single-handedly produced a completed design, ready to manufacture. The resulting floating point board was incredibly fast, much faster than the old one. It was even cheaper to build. Rich's accomplishment was remarkable.

In January, 1989, Multiflow introduced the new 300 Trace product series, the only change from the 200 series being Rich's floating point board. They provided free upgrades on all the machines in the field—not just to Motorola. And all the Traces, new and existing, went even faster.

* * *

Josh thought the price of the Multiflow Trace was too high, but he could never convince Don. Even though Don had organized Multiflow into a real company and ridden the engineers until they produced a great machine, now that it was in the marketplace, Josh had doubts about Don's judgment. He was afraid that all Don's experience, everything that made him so good at the start of the company, was holding them back. That all the knowledge of the seasoned professional wasn't right for pricing and selling the innovative VLIW technology. Josh was afraid that the lack of creativity he didn't think would be a problem when he recruited a "white socks engineer" to be Multiflow's CEO was catching up with them.

Don was a computer industry veteran with decades of experience telling him how pricing should work. He used industry guidelines which said to spend x% on marketing, y% on presales support, and so on—and this was Don's bible. If the quarterly margin numbers were high, Don thought he was doing his job—short-term profits had always been the goal of all of his Boards of Directors. And he believed that prices should be as high as possible to keep those margins high. He didn't see spending money or reducing prices as investing in the future of Multiflow, as Josh argued; he just saw that his margin numbers would go down. Going forward, always upward, was business ethic number one.

It was the same with the sales force which Don's people hired. The salesmen were experienced; they knew how to sell conventional computers barely different from the competition, not products where the customer needed to believe in innovative technology. They were paid through a combination of salary, commissions, and bonuses for making targets, which made them want to keep the prices up: the higher the prices, the more money they made.

But Josh thought that the conventional sales compensation structure was all wrong for Multiflow because they needed to do so much more proving than companies with conventional technology. In addition to the salespeople, they had to send sales support staff to visit prospects, to show them how their programs would run on the Trace. Sending the support people out was expensive, but Josh thought it was the only sales expense they should have. He thought they should eliminate most of the salesmen—concentrating on marketing and support instead.

John O'Donnell agreed with Josh. They had both been in the field, had seen how sales prospects approached VLIW technology, seen the fear. It took a lot of trust for a company to spent half a million dollars on a computer, even more trust to buy an untested technology. They came across customers who fully understood that the Trace would go four times as fast as their present computers for half the price but who wouldn't consider buying a Trace. If the old one was doing the job, they were afraid to change, saw no reason to risk their jobs on a possible improvement.

"No one ever got fired for recommending IBM," the saying went, and Multiflow came across many customers who lived by it.

In the 1980s, Mazda advertised its Wankel rotary engine as a feature of its cars. The ads were compelling, with a catchy jingle, and people who bought Mazdas loved the smoothness and power. But too few people bought the cars; the innovative technology never attracted customers—and discouraged far too many who were afraid of the engine. They wouldn't flock to an untested, new technology they didn't know anything about. Mazda made high-end cars with the Wankel engine until quite recently, but they stopped advertising it a long time ago.

This was the mentality Josh was going against, and he and O'Donnell believed strongly that Multiflow needed a more aggressive pricing strategy to fight it. Multiflow was already priced lower than the competition, much lower when you took into account how much faster they were, but Josh and O'Donnell thought that pushing prices lower still would make a difference. They each believed this independently, both having had the same experiences in the field. And they argued furiously with Don over pricing, separately and together.

The Trace cost between $300k and $700k, depending on how it was configured and how hard the customer bargained. If, instead, the company sold reasonably configured computers for $250k, Multiflow could be profitable, though barely. But they would get lots of machines out in the field, the manufacturing line would be humming, and there would be buzz everywhere from satisfied customers. Josh thought that if they had 75 happy customers in the first eighteen months of product availability, they would have a customer base they could build on, despite minimal profits. When there were enough people using the new technology, they could raise their prices. With greater volume, manufacturing costs would come down and, little by little, they would become profitable. With flat prices which they wouldn't negotiate, they wouldn't spend as much on sales because they wouldn't become involved in protracted presales battles.

But Don wouldn't hear any of it, dismissing their concerns. Why should he listen to children like them who didn't know anything about the industry? He was the veteran. Just because they said that the industry was changing and VLIW technology was different, this was not enough for him to pay attention. He didn't isolate Josh and John because he respected their abilities; he just ignored them, making them furious. They didn't even consider taking the pricing issue to the Board of Directors. It would have been futile; they always deferred to Don on questions like this.

I followed the pricing controversy as Josh brought his worries home, sad to see Josh pulling away from Don on such an important issue. And the disagreement was painful. Don had been so good for the company when it started; Josh was used to agreeing with him, seeing eye-to-eye. But now Josh and O'Donnell thought the pricing and selling strategy wasn't smart enough, that marketing and sales were not up to the quality of the engineering. This was a separation that had never been part of Multiflow before; the engineers and Don's people were now seeing things differently.

Were Josh and John right? How could they be so arrogant to think they were? This was the same presumptuousness that made Josh believe he knew how to design a computer better than the computer science community, now applied to an industry veteran. Josh was right then—the Trace went blazingly fast. Were he and

O'Donnell right in believing that the computer industry was changing, becoming more price sensitive, and that Multiflow had to follow a different path to succeed?

Instead of lowering prices Don suggested they market a slower, lower priced product for people who couldn't afford the current one—a 7/300 with a slower clock. He wanted to fill out the product line and get a foothold at the low end of the market; he thought that once customers got a look, they would be more receptive to the higher priced machine.

But the hardware engineers went crazy at the idea of slowing down the clock. They hated it. They had labored to make the Trace incredibly fast and now they had to slow it down? They thought it was insulting to them and brutally unfair to the customer to give them less than the computer could do. The customer had the machine, and now he couldn't work it to its full potential? They thought it was just wrong: Josh was afraid that Papworth and Rodman might quit because they were so mad.

Josh was startled by this strong reaction. Why did he think it was okay to slow down the clock, yet the engineers didn't? Multiflow wasn't out to cheat the customer. He finally decided that the problem must be a difference of approach. Like so many others, the engineers were thinking only about hardware and not looking at the whole product, not considering that what they were selling was the intellectual property.

"When you buy software, like Microsoft Word, the floppy disk costs a dollar," Josh told them. "Why should they charge more than two dollars? And why are there different versions of Word, some more capable than others, all with different prices? The floppy still costs a dollar to make.

"What we're selling is intellectual property that speeds up the computer," he continued. "The only way we can have a range of products to sell is to let the customer decide how much intellectual property he wants to buy. Slowing the clock gives us a cheaper product to sell, and it's not unfair to the customer. We are telling them exactly what we are doing. Since we are delivering a processor along with our intellectual property, we can control how fast it goes. If they want it to be faster, they can get a field upgrade later to a 300 series, if that's what they want to do."

That calmed Papworth and Rodman down a little. At least they understood the logic. And Multiflow developed the Trace 7/100—simply the 7/300 slowed down. They put in a slower clock, reducing the number of cycles per second, and made a few other changes so that the customer couldn't speed up the processing. Otherwise, it was the same machine.

* * *

International sales were another area of bitter contention between Josh and Don, Josh favoring rapid expansion overseas, while Don was focused only on the US market. O'Donnell agreed with Josh here, too, but not as adamantly as on pricing. On the international issue, most often, Josh argued alone.

Multiflow's first international distributor had come to them easily, without their having to do anything. This was Mike Emrich, who ran GEI, a division of Daimler-Benz, a German computer distributor headquartered in Aachen. He was very aggressive and Multiflow was lucky to get him. Mike had read the *Business Week* article and sat down with Josh at the Santa Clara product introduction. Looking at the Trace, he quickly decided that GEI needed to distribute it. They signed an agreement, Multiflow shipped computers assembled in Branford and GEI began selling.

Josh thought this was great, that they needed to get more distributors like Mike. He talked to Don, but again found that what he was suggesting wasn't conventional wisdom.

"Yeah, yeah; we'll get to it. We need to build a solid company in the US before we start worrying about anything foreign," said Don.

"Xenophobia!" yelled Josh, upset at what he saw as small-minded thinking.

Josh found articles describing EU economic power and showed them to anyone who would listen. This time Josh did go to the Board, arguing that Multiflow's future depended on opening up international sales far more aggressively than they were doing. The European Union would soon have its own currency and become a single market. He said they had to go in there now; there were opportunities in this exploding market that they couldn't afford to miss. But the Board shared Don's America-centric view. They had traveled and thought of Paris as a great place for a meal, but anyplace outside the US was a secondary market.

Mike Emrich was the one voice supporting Josh. Convex—Multiflow's principal competitor—could raise prices all they wanted in the territories where they had no competition, often double the US price—enabling them to lower prices in the US and Germany—and GEI's prices were constantly being undercut. And over half of Convex's sales were coming from places where they could make those sky-high profits. Josh wanted Multiflow to be wherever Convex was, and he argued the point adamantly. It wasn't good for Multiflow to let their major competitor stay unopposed this way. Convex wouldn't be able to undercut Mike if they had competition in the rest of Europe.

Bob Smith, VP of Sales and Marketing, understood the competitive situation and wanted to hire salesmen around the world. Josh liked the distributor model better and because he pushed so hard, they ended up doing both. In France, Josh and Bob Buchanan, Director of Marketing, found Metrologie and signed them up as their French distributor. They were more difficult than GEI, arrogant and fussy, but they arranged for Josh to meet the French press and customers. And Multiflow signed an Israeli distribution agreement with Unipower, as well.

Josh signed up an Italian distributor, but it took endless negotiations, dragging on for more than a year. This was Delphi, a subsidiary of Olivetti, just winding down their computer operations in the US. It got to the point that everyone at Multiflow laughed at Josh, telling him he was wasting his time because it was obvious to them that the CEO of Olivetti Systems, Elserino Piol, was just stringing him along. Even I laughed at Josh, teasing that Olivetti was the Italian lover he couldn't stop meeting. Josh was frustrated, too, but Delphi did, finally, become Multiflow's Italian distributor, responsible for the sale in Catania which brought Josh to the Italian Parliament. They sold other computers, too, including one to the trucking division of Fiat.

And Multiflow found a Japanese distributor, C. Itoh, an important Japanese printer company. On a sales trip to Japan that he made with Bob Smith, Josh gave his talk three times in the same room, as customers paraded by. Then, in the evening, C. Itoh took them to a banquet at a private club where they were served by geishas, to the delight of the junior people who didn't get to do this often.

The senior people asked Josh about the translator, a freelancer, educated in the US. Because of her obvious competence, the C. Itoh executives wondered if they should consider hiring her. Josh had also been impressed by her; he could tell she was good because of the way her speed varied at the complicated spots in the technical descriptions, but sped up with each repetition. But since she had told Josh that she would never work for a Japanese company because of the way they treated women, he didn't think it would be a good match. And, sure enough, when he said that she seemed like an "independent thinker," a veil came down over the executives' eyes. They decided they wouldn't think about hiring her after all.

RISC から VLIW へ
コンパイラ主導の開発が鍵に

Joseph A . Fisher 氏（米 Multiflow Computer, Inc. 副社長）

まずコンパイラを書き，次にそれに合ったコンピュータを設計した。 VLIWの
生みの親，米 Multiflow Computer, Inc. の Joseph A. Fisher 副社長に，VLIW
開発の経緯とその位置付けを聞いた。VLIW は，RISC を一歩進めたコンピュー
タ・アーキテクチャ。512ビット幅などの命令を使い，1命令で複数の演算を
同時実行する。科学技術計算などの処理速度を上げるには有効である。ただし，
コンパイラの最適化が必須で，コンパイラ主導の開発になった。

With all these distribution deals, Multiflow seemed poised to jump into international sales. Bob hired Chris Chaney to run the European operation, supporting the distributors and managing salesmen in territories not covered by distributorships: the UK, Belgium and the Netherlands. The European sales office was about to open; Chris's salesmen should start selling soon. And Josh hoped that revenue from international sales would make up for US sales which were lower than he thought they should be.

DOLDRUMS

By mid-1987 Multiflow had raised almost $36 million in three rounds of financing, and money was coming in from sales, but it wasn't enough. With sales revenues not as high as they had projected, the company needed money—and sources were drying up.

After the mezzanine round of financing—the third round—the usual next step for a start-up was going public. But to go public in those days, you needed to be profitable; you couldn't ask people to buy shares in your company when not enough customers were buying your product. The VCs bought private shares, of course, before the public offering, but that was speculation. When you sold common stock, you needed something more solid.

They might have been able to get another round of financing together in normal times, but the investment climate had turned mean. On Monday, October 19, 1987, stock markets worldwide crashed, with the Dow Jones average falling over five hundred points in a single day—an unheard-of decline at the time. Overnight VCs stopped investing; the effect on start-up businesses was as bad as the dot-com bust twelve years later. Another round of financing was out of the question.

Instead, Multiflow turned to R&D partnerships and other odd ways of raising money. They talked to other computer companies, looking for investments, partnerships—any way to get additional money. Josh and many of the engineers favored a partnership with DEC where they knew a lot of people. DEC was interested in Multiflow as a technical partner and Josh spent a lot of time courting them, but negotiations didn't move along as quickly as he had expected.

The Wallonian region of Belgium—the French speaking southern half—invested $4 million in Multiflow in exchange for the company's agreement to locate its European headquarters in the region. Also, the State of Connecticut invested around $2 million in a networking project. And Prudential bought royalties, patents and ownership interest in the next Trace product, a machine with faster hardware, for about $12 million. Intel also made a technology investment, about $2 million, with options for a lot more, getting VLIW consulting and collaboration in return. But without the sales to support the operation, even these investments were not enough to turn Multiflow into a financially stable company.

And at the same time Multiflow was having money trouble, the computer industry was changing and these changes created problems. In the 1970s and early 1980s, no one cared that computers were incompatible, that programs that ran on one company's computers couldn't run on any other. Compatible computers were denigrated and called clones—as though the manufacturer didn't have the creativity to come up with something original, and most manufacturers changed architectures willingly. Apple, for instance, marketed its IIe computers heavily to schools and parents; after it was a big hit with educators, they blew it all away by introducing the incompatible Macintosh.

Now, as the industry evolved, object code incompatibility started to look like a flaw. And since the essence of VLIW technology is that the hardware and the software look alike, incompatibility was fundamental to the product, nothing that could be engineered out. And unlike computers which were incompatible with other company's products, but compatible with products made by the same manufacturer, Trace code was incompatible among Trace models. You couldn't run code compiled for the 200 series on the 300 series, and 7/300 code had to be recompiled to perform well on a 14/300.

Also, computer hardware itself was changing, becoming cheaper, making it easier to produce powerful machines. The number of transistors that could be put on an integrated circuit doubled every two years—Moore's Law—and Intel introduced chips with entire CPUs on them. The smaller the chips were, the shorter the distance the electrical impulse has to travel, speeding up processing. Personal computers, which had limited technical use when Multiflow started, became more powerful—and they were compatible across manufacturers. Because PCs could run many scientific applications, the entire mini-supercomputer industry was threatened. This was the "Attack of the Killer Micros" that people started to talk about, including John Markoff in *The New York Times*.

These were the years when Steve Jobs raised $350 million to start NeXT, almost six times as much as Multiflow, ultimately failing to take over the industry. There were so many companies manufacturing mini-supercomputers now that the market was saturated and Multiflow's competitors started to go out of business. Analysts predicted that the market would eventually shake out to only three companies: Alliant, Convex and Multiflow.

Because of price pressure from the killer micros and the casualties among competitors, Josh redoubled his efforts to get Don to reduce prices and to push foreign marketing to the top of his list. Both issues seemed more urgent now. The arguments grew more bitter and the breach more open. The Board was losing confidence in Don, too, over the sluggish sales. Don had been so wonderful, a great engineering manager when the company was getting going; they owed their professionalism to him. Now he and Josh saw the company completely differently.

When Josh made hiring decisions, he always looked for employees not afraid to contradict him. He thrived on challenge, all the engineers did, throwing themselves against the hardest problems and putting their intelligence to work. A disagreement was an opportunity to improve—it was the way of science. But it didn't seem to be the way in business. Josh increasingly believed that the financial, administrative and sales divisions were not up to the standard the engineers set at Multiflow. He thought Don hired people who agreed with him, not aiming for the best minds.

And it was true: Don hired people who shared his approach, people who could be relied on to agree with him, not only in marketing and in sales, but in the financial, manufacturing and administrative divisions as well. These were sweet people, a lot of them, but not people who would stand up to Don when they needed to. Sometimes it seemed like Leigh was the only big thinker outside of the technical group, and he was left over from the pre-Don era. Don even got rid of Brian Cohen, the genius publicist responsible for the product introduction at the World Trade Center and all the great early publicity, because his innovative thinking annoyed Bob Smith. Without Brian, Multiflow staged a droney product introduction in Branford featuring disco lights.

Josh was also appalled at the sky-high compensation of the people Don hired. He didn't know and couldn't accept how much more valuable the business world thought they were than the genius engineers working on the product. Many of the marketing people were paid far more in salary than John O'Donnell, something Josh simply couldn't understand. And when Don gave an outside director, Peter Lyman, a scientist from the Jet Propulsion Laboratory, more Multiflow stock than Bob Nix, who was crucial to the success of the Trace, Josh was horrified. The engineers shared Josh's distress, outraged that Don had created nine vice presidents at such a small company.

"Did he think we wouldn't notice?" asked Bob Colwell, expressing the concern they all shared.

The problems between Don and Josh became so bad in late 1988 that Josh talked to Felda Hardymon about his replacing Don as CEO. Felda was one of Multiflow's original investors, on the Board from the start.

Josh made a concerted pitch one evening when the three of us were out for dinner, telling Felda about his ideas for the company and how they differed from Don's. I was shocked, not expecting this, but I was quiet, since I didn't want to contradict him. If Josh had asked me, I would have told him how appalled I was at the idea of him as CEO. When I saw how stressed he was now, I dreaded what would happen if he pushed harder. Despite Multiflow's problems, this didn't seem like the answer to me.

Josh backed off quickly, realizing how inappropriate it was for him to be suggesting fundamental company changes at a social dinner.

"And he brings his wife!" Josh said, describing the absurdity of what he was doing.

Felda was the VC Josh felt most comfortable with, who believed in his technology from the very beginning. But when even he couldn't see Josh as CEO of Multiflow, Josh dropped the subject.

* * *

For a while it seemed like everything was going wrong. In 1988, John O'Donnell got sick and rumors circulated that he was having a nervous breakdown. He had thrown himself into building Multiflow, body and mind, never resting; a breakdown seemed like a natural consequence. John would be out sick for a week, then struggle in for a few days, showing the O'Donnell magic, and then be out another week. It was a crisis, even though Bob Nix took over most of his responsibilities and the hardware guys could manage on their own. John's energy, vision and drive were central to the company and everyone counted on him.

At first John's doctors couldn't find anything wrong with him. But finally, he found that he had chronic Lyme disease, a newly discovered condition then. He lived only thirty miles from Lyme, CT, and when the tick carrying the disease bit him, John had been taking antibiotics for a different condition, so the characteristic rash didn't appear. The disease retreated into his body, debilitating him, causing him problems no one could get to the bottom of. Once John got an accurate diagnosis and was treated with intravenous antibiotics, he got back on his feet. And in true John O'Donnell fashion, he threw himself into Lyme disease research, writing scholarly papers to add to medical knowledge. But it took a year before John was back at full strength.

And then there were the layoffs.

"You guys are way out ahead of what you need on staffing from where you should be," some of the VCs said.

And it was partly true. Multiflow identified a small number of less essential new hires and let them go, mostly administrative people. That was relatively painless.

The second layoff was worse, this one eating much farther into the company. They lost ten percent of the employees, about twenty people, including a tech writer, some marketing and salespeople who hadn't been producing enough, and one hardware engineer who had lived in his office for over a year. They lost some loveable people who had been part of the company for a long time—and it hurt.

The next thing to go wrong was a theft. Since many people had to go in and out of the locked metal parts cage on the manufacturing floor, they hadn't kept close watch on the keys. No one worried; who in this group could possibly be a problem? Everyone at Multiflow knew and liked each other; it felt like a family.

Then one day several thousand dollars worth of memory chips were missing from the parts cage. They scoured Multiflow, then called the police. Since all the stolen parts had serial numbers, they hoped the chips would turn up for sale. But the stolen chips never surfaced; they never heard anything more and it demoralized everyone. The spirit of the company made it seem as though a theft couldn't happen—but it did.

The parts theft really cut into Josh's heart. He remembered teaching at Brooklyn College in the 1970s, when some of his students had cheated on an exam. He was close to those students, not much older than they were; they enjoyed the same things. Josh brought a lot of himself into his classes. And when some of those students cheated on his exams, it wounded him to his core.

"When you go into the money economy, you have to expect things like that," Martin, our wise friend, told him then.

It was the same thing here, but it was very painful. Josh had a picture of a Multiflow in his mind where everyone worked together for the common good. Now that picture was diminished.

There were other problems, too. A secretary working for Leigh was killed in a car accident one night. She was in her early twenties; it was a terrible tragedy and everyone mourned. And there were Multiflow divorces—O'Donnell, Bob Nix and Bob Smith—all of them putting too much of themselves into the company, not taking enough time with their families.

Josh was overworked, too. He didn't exercise, stopped playing squash and began putting on weight, making him feel bloated and out of shape. He paid attention to his family in those years and went to the doctor regularly but, outside of those things, he neglected everything else.

And I was having problems, too, pains in my wrist that I didn't understand. For years I had produced slides on the computer, typed papers for my MBA classes and written exams by hand—all under tremendous time pressure. The result was constant pain, and I didn't know how to make it stop. Combing five year-old Dorothy's hair was excruciating, so much so that I had it cut short.

Since computers were only then coming into general use, repetitive strain injury problems were very new. My doctor had never seen one before, but he was hearing about them. When he told me what he thought was going wrong, I began to realize how ergonomically poor my wonderful digitizer was. The stylus I pushed down on to enter data put pressure on my wrist with every stroke. But I loved this machine, loved working fast—seemingly

217

magically—to produce complicated pictures. There was no way I was giving it up; I could never go back to a mouse.

My doctor filled me with anti-inflammatory drugs and prescribed a wrist brace—then he began to talk about surgery. I listened, took the medicine and wore the brace. But I wasn't ready to consider anything drastic.

Not everything at Multiflow was demoralizing in these years. The younger employees continued to have babies, and there were Multiflow marriages, too, to offset the divorces. Joanne McIntyre, Josh's secretary after his secretary from Yale moved into administration, married John Brown who managed the Multiflow installations. Holly Biertempfel, a tech writer laid off in the second round, married Dave Long in tech support. And Bob Nix and John O'Donnell both remarried, John marrying the Jewish chaplain at Wesleyan University. Josh suggested that when they got married Drorah should change her name and become Rabbi O'Donnell because, amusingly, the Wesleyan Catholic chaplain was Father Cohen.

And favorable press coverage continued unabated, Multiflow's financial problems unknown. Many publications that hadn't gotten on the bandwagon in the first wave of publicity saw Multiflow press releases and fell all over themselves with praise.

Josh learned to expect that most newspapers and magazines would print the press releases without any effort to verify the claims. At first this startled him, since he had had faith in press independence. Then he came to accept it and began looking at all news with skepticism, giving him a permanent cynicism about the media.

When people congratulated me, I knew better than to hint at company problems because this might become self-fulfilling, creating a domino effect to drive Multiflow under. The whole thing gave me the willies, though. I thought it was crazy to paint the company as glamorous now that it was having trouble. Where were all these people in Multiflow's early years when the future seemed so unlimited? That's what I wanted to know.

* * *

In late 1988, it began to look as though Multiflow had no future. The numbers just didn't add up. There was no business plan that made sense; they needed a new strategy. When they looked for fresh money now, they were looking in unconventional directions.

One of the VCs knew a company with a lot of money in search of a product: a company with a dowry. This was Adage, an old workstation manufacturer that had mostly ceased operation. All they had left was a service business for their old products—but they had $10 million in the bank. The VC thought it would be a good match, each company having something the other wanted.

Negotiations went on for some time and in March, 1989, Multiflow and Adage announced an agreement. Subject to shareholder approval, the two companies would merge in a stock swap, the new company being called Multiflow. Adage would have 40% of the voting stock and the former Multiflow 60%. The Adage CEO, Jim Norrod, would become the Multiflow CEO and Don, who at age 66 was ready for a smaller role, would become Chairman of the Board. They expected the merger to be finalized within 120 days.

Of course Josh knew Multiflow was in trouble and needed money, but he didn't like this deal. Something about Jim Norrod rubbed him the wrong way; Josh found him untrustworthy. And when he thought about the company that would result from the merger, he wondered if it would still be the place he loved. Multiflow was moving away from him; he didn't think there would be a role in the management of the new company for him. And he figured that if he wasn't going to become Multiflow CEO, and the merger was really going to happen, then he had better get out of the way.

European sales were Josh's highest priority now, and he thought he should turn his energies there. The whole international operation needed leverage and to be kick-started. Other than Germany, none of the distributors was up and running yet. They were having choppy starts and the Belgian headquarters was slow to get going.

If Josh moved to Europe and worked with the sales force there he could add energy and move it along. He had been directly involved in most of the first US sales; he could do the same thing in Europe. And he could keep watch on the Wallonian agreement, too, which looked as though it needed closer management.

The contract with the Wallonian Region was negotiated at the very end of the period when venture-funded technology start-ups were hot; the charismatic Premier, wanting to modernize the region, had decided to get on the bandwagon. The agreement required Multiflow to set up its European marketing headquarters and a transit facility in Wallonia. It provided cash at set milestones: an initial investment; another when the headquarters was announced; another when it was established, and so on. It would be good for Wallonia—providing jobs—and good for Multiflow, providing investment dollars and cash incentives.

Both sides signed the agreement and Wallonia sent the initial payment. Multiflow announced its European headquarters and waited for the next payment, due to be paid then. When it didn't arrive promptly, Multiflow wasn't concerned and moved on to the next milestone, renting headquarters space in Louvain-la-Neuve, a lovely university town about twenty miles south of Brussels. They waited for the next payment. And waited again.

Now the Wallonian government was two payments behind and Multiflow started to worry. They checked back with Philippe DeVille, who ran the technology office, but didn't get satisfactory answers. The government had recently changed and the new administration was less friendly to the idea of technology investment. But Multiflow had a signed contract and had fulfilled all its obligations; they expected that Wallonia would live up to its part of the bargain.

EUROPE

Calvin Trillin says that children are ready to visit Europe when they are willing to eat a mushroom. By this measure, our kids were unprepared for life abroad and, although I passed the mushroom test, I wasn't ready either.

A lot has been written about culture shock, the personal disorientation of an unfamiliar way of life, but in 1989, I had never heard of it. I rushed into international living with a naïve optimism and then stopped abruptly, confounded by what I found. I didn't realize that just below the part that tourists see, there is a world so unlike what I was used to that it made me question many of my basic assumptions. I felt like Alice, falling down the rabbit hole.

Today the homogenizing effects of the internet and globalization have brought the world closer together; the French don't even smoke in restaurants any more. Back then, though, I found the differences stark and, until I got used to it, profoundly unsettling.

* * *

With the Adage deal set to close at Multiflow and his own role uncertain, Josh suggested that our whole family move to Brussels, near Multiflow European headquarters where he could support the European sales efforts.

"I hate being away from you and the kids so much," he said. "If we move, I can go to meetings there and still be near you—coming home at night."

The suggestion came out of nowhere and I had to let it sink in. I knew Josh was concerned about Multiflow's neglect of international sales, but I had no idea this was in his mind.

"We can stay a year, maybe as much as three—as long as it takes for the European operation to stand on its own." Josh continued outlining his plan. "I'll have to go back to the States sometimes but, because of Adage, it shouldn't be that often. We'd like it, and think how educational it would be for the kids—they'd get to see Europe."

I was in my last semester of MBA studies, getting my degree in January, so the timing was right for me. I liked the idea of Josh's being home more; the kids and I really missed him when he was away. They were still young, not teenagers who would be hard to uproot. And I loved traveling in Europe. It seemed like a great adventure—for all of us.

"Yes," I said. "Let's do it."

In April 1989, we took the kids on a house-hunting trip to Brussels—the first time they'd been outside the US. I tried to prepare them, explaining that Belgians spoke French or Flemish, but that many people spoke English. The customs were different, more formal than what they were used to, but no one would make them do anything they were uncomfortable with. We would look at a lot of homes and schools, and settle where we could all be happy. We would be able to do what we needed to do; it would just take a little patience.

We took a red-eye to Brussels and the cheery relocation guy, Eric Klitch—"Your Friend in Belgium"—met us at the airport. He brought the kids and me to the apartment we had rented for the week while Josh took another flight to Geneva for a meeting at CERN, the European organization for nuclear research. I went out to the grocery store and tried to make sense of where I was.

On my trips to Europe, I had always stayed at hotels, eaten in restaurants and talked to people used to working with traveling foreigners. Now, though, I found that away from the tourist areas things were different. I didn't recognize the products on the grocery store shelves and I hadn't recognized the appliances in the apartment kitchen, either. I was surprised at how few people spoke English, and my college language skills weren't as strong as I had thought.

The next morning, with Josh back, Eric Klitch picked us up, and we began the job we had come to Brussels to do—finding a place to live and a school for the kids. We all liked the International School of Brussels and the kids breathed a sigh of relief. They had been upset by a bi-lingual Belgian school we visited where the students had the choice of having beer or milk with their meals. When the teachers spoke to them in French, they were so horrified that they risked being rude, something Josh and I had cautioned them against, by whispering frantically that this was not the school for them.

The ISB roughly followed the American curriculum, although it was famous for elaborate field trips supplementing the class work. Most of the students came from outside Belgium, but not all of them were Americans. The kids' classmates' parents were diplomats, executives of multinational corporations, and a few NATO officials, though most of the military children went to school on the base. Everyone at the ISB spoke English and no one got beer at lunch.

We rented a house just outside the city center in the Commune of Woluwe St. Pierre. A few blocks away there was a baker and other food shops and there was a Centre Sportif where the kids could swim. The house was just off a main street where a tram ran to a nearby market square. The ISB was a twenty minute drive away.

The master bedroom in the house was on the main floor and, oddly, the master bath didn't include a toilet—that was in the front of the house, along with a sink. The kids' bedrooms were upstairs; Dorothy's room had a Juliet balcony, and downstairs there was a glassed-in study for our computer equipment. There was even a backyard for our dog Rosie, a Brittany Spaniel. The house was furnished, somewhat shabbily; all we had to do was bring our personal possessions.

Dorothy and me in front of the Brussels house

Back in the States, we prepared to move to Europe, but just as we were about to leave, the Adage deal fell apart. It had been approved by their Board of Directors, but some of the principal shareholders decided that Multiflow was not a good investment. Suddenly, Multiflow was turned upside down again. Adage was to have funded operations.

So, now what? European sales were more important than ever—but so was the DEC deal—the technology partnership with the Digital Equipment Corporation that Josh had been working on in Massachusetts. With Adage set to close, DEC had been on the back burner, but now it was the next most likely source of investment capital. Josh had expected to separate himself from Multiflow in the States when had he planned the European move, but would that be possible now? European sales and the DEC deal—he needed to do both at once. We decided to go ahead with our move.

Many Multiflow engineers were confused about Josh's going to Europe, the value of sales support being a hard concept for scientists. Some people thought he was being kicked upstairs and some thought it was the reward of a European vacation. And the failure of the Adage merger brought out the worst in some people.

"Don told me that he finally found a way to get rid of Fisher," Jim Norrod, the Adage CEO, said to Josh as his parting shot.

Was that true? Did Don want to get rid of Josh—sending him to Europe? Or was Norrod being vindictive? Don and Josh had differences, but going to Europe was Josh's idea—the way he thought he could be the most use. He didn't know what to think about the crack from Norrod, but it left a bad taste in his mouth.

Just before we moved to Brussels, Josh's friends at Multiflow gave a party for us at Woody Lichtenstein's home, a potluck with everyone bringing the food they cooked best. John and Margie Ruttenberg brought cases of Champagne, Margie joking that it was *her* best dish. It was a wonderful party, full of celebration of the Multiflow Josh and I had loved for so long. These were the people I cared about; the ones whose creative energies made it the special place it was. I relaxed, letting out a breath I didn't know I was holding. With all the frenzy of leaving, I had been tensing up all the muscles in my body and the party overwhelmed me with warmth.

* * *

We moved to Brussels in mid-May 1989, to the little house on Avenue de Gomrée in Woluwe St. Pierre. When we arrived, we got off our red-eye, got to the house, and Josh went to meet with Chris Chaney, the European Sales Manager, leaving me to unpack and organize. The next day the kids started school at the ISB; the bus picked them up two blocks away.

Left in the house, I was dazed, all the differences that had struck me on our house-hunting trip hitting again, hard. Every one of them was small but they added up, creating a feeling of disorientation that threatened to overwhelm me. Why did all these little things bother me so much?—it wasn't making any sense. Usually I was adaptable and I had wanted to move to Brussels. I was looking forward to my new life; I wanted this adventure.

But it took me a long time to adjust and it was very tiring. All the everyday parts of my life were different. My papers from home didn't fit anywhere since European paper sizes are different, nor did our sheets fit the beds. The food, though delicious, was unfamiliar, and to cook it I had to translate Celsius into Fahrenheit and use kitchen appliances that looked as though they came from Mars. The laundry took hours and seemed to grind the clothes into bits. And doing almost everything outside the house while speaking French was exhausting, the necessary concentration causing a tension that was hard to turn off. I ended up feeling like I was speaking French all night in my sleep.

The differences went much deeper than language, too, as I discovered when one helpful person stopped to give me directions. He kindly pointed straight ahead while saying "always right, always right," translating the French "tout droit" literally. And beyond simple translation, I had to learn a more evasive form of conversation, in both languages—where "yes" didn't always mean "yes."

It wasn't just the place and the people that were different, either. All the administration necessary to run a household were hard to negotiate. It took us weeks to get a telephone and, at first, Josh had to conduct business from a phone booth a block away. And it also took weeks for us to be able to get to our money.

"It's stuck in foreign exchange," bank officials told us over and over. "We'd be happy to loan you some money if you need it right away..."

I got mad, yelling, "It's my money!" and hopping around. But it got me nowhere.

Dorothy, the most verbal of children at age seven, found it frightening not to be able to communicate. In the grocery store, she wandered off when I wasn't looking, and I found her two aisles over, frightened, asking everyone she saw whether they spoke English. Soon, though, she found a group of classmates she cared about: girls from England, Egypt, India, Peru, and Mexico, as well as from the US. They became inseparable, this large group of girls protecting each other against the new world they were all experiencing.

Dave didn't have as easy a time finding friends as Dorothy did; most of the boys in his class had led international lives from the start and didn't share his interest in science and math. They were much more sophisticated, having girlfriends in the fifth grade, and Dave had little in common with them. And the pace was a problem for him, too. The first week he was at the ISB, his class took a trip to the science museum in Eindhoven, in the Netherlands, a couple of hours away. Then, two weeks later, they took a week-long field trip to Trier, Germany, to study Roman ruins, exploring by day and doing rigorous homework by night. It was breathtakingly fast.

But by the next fall, when Dave's sixth-grade class took a weeklong trip to Florence to study art, science and history of the Renaissance, he was up to speed. He liked it so much that when Josh went to a conference in Pisa a month later, our whole family went along, stopping for a few days in Florence for Dave to show us what he had learned.

As the kids got used to it, I got used to it too, taking it in stride when Dave came home with tales of the outing his school had been on without the formality of a permission slip. I joined a French class at the ISB, a continuing class that met twice a week, and the women in this class became my community. They were all trailing spouses like me, wives who needed to learn the language and didn't know the customs. In French, we discussed how to work through our daily lives, what we were supposed to be doing and how to do it.

I started shopping at the three-day-a-week market at the end of the street, lining up for my produce at the farmers with the longest lines—the good farmers—considering them as reliable as merchants in stores, letting them pick out my vegetables, not presuming to touch. I had my favorites, waiting for the best mushroom man to appear, the best cheese man, not accepting substitutes. I learned to buy smaller amounts of food, too, since the refrigerator was so small. And I learned to use a fish knife—something I had never seen before—from the copy of *Miss Manners* that I asked Josh to bring back with him on one of his trips to the States.

When my friend Evelyn Rudahl visited over Thanksgiving, she taught me about the vegetables and other unfamiliar food at the markets. She was born in Germany, her parents German immigrants to the US, and she recognized a lot from her childhood; cooking got a lot easier with her help. And the food was amazingly wonderful, the butter richer and more creamy than American butter, the chicken and vegetables somehow more flavorful. The bread was indescribably good. And when Josh's parents visited, my mother-in-law, Sue, told me that the egg yolks looked and tasted as rich as those she remembered from her childhood—but hadn't seen since.

I liked using grams right away; 100 grams seemed about right for a snack. And a demi-kilo was about an American pound. But I hated Celsius; the degrees were so big that I couldn't see how anyone could tell the real temperature. And it took me a while to get a feeling for kilometers.

"They have cute little countries in Europe," Josh said, "and they have cute little miles, too. That's the way to think of it."

I got it then, forever—for me, a kilometer became a miniature version of a mile.

A milkman delivered our milk to a box at the door and he also brought cases of Badoit, the mineral-tasting sparkling water Josh loved. And for meat and bread, I went to the shops a few blocks from us when they first opened, asking questions when the owners had time to be patient with me. And I learned to expect that small businesses closed for two hours in the middle of the day for lunch, saving me the wasted trips that I'd had when we first moved to Brussels.

And I got used to the European idea, common in those days, that bathing too frequently was bad for the body. All the houses had bidets, and other odors—"good human smells"—were not considered offensive. Because the laundry was so harsh, Europeans didn't wash clothes as often as I was used to, either; body odors became part of my environment—along with the idea that chocolate was a health food.

When we first got to Brussels, we rented cars before our leased cars were ready. Josh's was a Citroen with pneumatic suspension and a single windshield wiper at the front windshield. He was charmed by this car and the kids loved to watch as it rose from the pavement while the suspension inflated. I called it "Josh's French mistress," though, pretty sure that all those quirks, which seemed so charming at first, would soon become irritating. Sure enough, Josh was more than ready when his sensible Audi arrived.

Events in Europe were startlingly close here; we felt as though we were living on top of history. Many of Dorothy's outgrown clothes were trucked to Romania as that country opened its borders when the Soviet Union collapsed. Then, the weekend after the Berlin Wall fell in November, I wanted to drive there—it was a real party as everyone descended on Berlin, close enough for us to get to easily. We finally decided that the traffic jams would keep us away, but the whole continent, including Brussels, was celebrating.

World War II ended in 1945 but in 1989, the Belgians still felt that it was the very recent past; there were a lot of preparations for forty-fifth anniversary celebrations the next year. Josh had always avoided the pain of learning about the Holocaust and his Jewish relatives caught in it, but when a tram conductor told him that the car he was riding on was used by the Nazis to transport prisoners, he decided he wanted to learn about the war. People everywhere pointed out landmarks to us, wanting to show us where battles happened, or how buildings in Brussels and all over Europe were used in the war. Josh's father was a World War II buff and, when he and Sue visited, we toured the site of the Battle of the Bulge in Bastogne and went to Anne Frank's house in Amsterdam. The shadow of the war felt very close.

Harry next to a World Wart II tank in Bastogne, Josh and Dave on top

We had a lot of visiting company and took many people to Bruges, the medieval city that is Belgium's most popular site. Then, on our own, we went to Paris or Cologne for weekends, traveled to German villages renowned for Christmas markets and to London. And we traveled down to the chateau country in the Loire valley of France and twice through Germany to Italy when Josh had business there, visiting the ski home of the Italian distributor on Mt. Blanc on our way back.

As we drove along, the kids alternated reading aloud from whatever book they were in the middle of—Ramona books for Dorothy; for several trips Dave was reading *Cheaper by the Dozen.*

"No more castles, no more cathedrals," they chanted. The kids would have liked staying home; they got pretty sick of the whole thing.

Josh and the kids in the Alps on our way to a conference in Pisa, November, 1989

When we first moved to Brussels, Josh found that potential customers didn't know who he was; outside of Germany, Multiflow was unknown. This took him back to his early days in the computer business, and he learned to go through the more elaborate introductions needed in Europe, finding contacts to introduce him. Soon, though, Josh and Chris Chaney opened the Multiflow European Headquarters in Louvain-La-Neuve, and Chris started arranging meetings. Josh visited that office occasionally, but he usually worked from our glassed-in home office when he wasn't on the road.

Josh was away on business a few days of most weeks, sometimes driving to GEI, the German distributor, just over the border in Aachen. When he went to Paris, he usually took the train in the early morning, having breakfast in the dining car along with other European business people going to meetings, waiters serving them as they sped by little European towns. And he went to Japan once, flying crammed into the smoking section of a Cathay Pacific plane whose seats were designed for smaller, Asian people.

Because the Adage merger failed, Josh wasn't able to completely separate himself from Multiflow in the States, and during the ten months we lived in Brussels, Josh returned thirteen times for work he couldn't delegate. And when he wasn't traveling, he was constantly conducting business on the phone. Even when his parents visited he had to stop at phone booths, spending our entire visit to Monet's gardens in Giverny, Sue's dream trip, on a conference call on a pay phone at the end of the garden.

On one trip, the only direct flight to the States that Josh could get on short notice left Europe from Amsterdam. When he arrived at the airport with only a small briefcase, he was sent into a separate room with about twenty other people, all of whom were being questioned carefully about their plans. He was held there for a long time—confusing him; he almost missing his plane to the States. Years later, the 9/11 attacks made him realize that his ticket purchased the same day and lack of luggage had triggered terrorism concerns, and that was why he had been held.

All this travel was tiring, especially the trips to the States, but Josh was accomplishing his goal in coming to Europe. The salesmen were selling, using his scientific expertise for back-up—and there were now distributors in all the more industrialized countries. And he was working with Bernard Amory, a local lawyer, getting the Walloonian Region to honor its contract. Coaxing that reluctant government to live up to its obligations was hard going but eventually they succeeded, bringing welcome money into Multiflow.

* * *

One evening Bernard invited Josh and me to a formal dinner party at his home along with seven other couples. My French class had been discussing these traditional occasions for weeks; now I got to go to one, entering a foreign home to see what it was really like. We brought cellophane wrapped flowers as I had been taught.

I had never seen anything like this party—elegance and formality I had only heard about. Everyone but us was in their thirties with young children at home; none of them was rich. Yet here was luxury I associated with much older people or wealth at the Ruttenberg level. According to my French teacher this was the way Belgians commonly socialized.

Following aperitifs and conversation, everyone sat down to dinner, a wonderful, elaborate French meal, cooked by an old woman, many courses with complex flavors. The cook remained in the kitchen with the door closed except to serve. We all sat and talked, enjoying the food. No one got up from the table; no one helped. And I sat entranced by this elegant world I had never seen before.

But I couldn't sit quietly; I had a role to play. The women around me were mostly administrative lawyers—solicitors, not barristers like Bernard. They were all smart, worldly women, but they didn't speak English. They had heard a lot about the US that made no sense to them, and they had been waiting for someone they could ask, someone who was willing to attempt the French and explain it to them—and that person was me. They were particularly interested in the American debate over abortion, then just beginning to hit the headlines.

Well, I tried. When Josh looked across the table at me, he thought he saw me speaking fluent French, gesturing for emphasis. But at my end, it didn't feel that way because I was trying to explain a hard problem in a language I barely understood. I saw myself thrashing, valiantly searching for words, trying to express subtle concepts in French with the vocabulary of a five year old child. Bernard, who spoke English, told me I was doing fine, but it didn't seem that way to me. I knew what I wanted to say, but I just didn't have the words. I kept starting sentences and trailing off. Using the wrong word, the wrong verb tense, not saying what was inside my head. I felt like Dorothy in the grocery store, talking to everyone in sight, desperate to find a way to communicate.

* * *

When we moved to Brussels, we brought all our computers and the Colormaster and digitizer so that Josh and I could continue to do presentation graphics. The Multiflow marketing department emailed me specifications, and I produced slides in bulk for the salespeople, the same way I did at home, sending them back with Josh or any Multifloid who happened to be in town. Occasionally I would transmit image files electronically, sending them across noisy international phone lines, but it was slow and rough in those early days. Once, when Josh forgot his presentation on a trip to London, it was touch and go whether he would get to give his talk. Each time the transmission failed, Josh called me back to suggest different modem settings for the next attempt—we tried them all, one by one. We succeeded, finally, and he got to give his talk, but it took hours to work through the transmission.

As I continued to produce slides, I had more wrist problems, the pain becoming so sharp I could barely do my work. My New Haven doctor suggested I come home for carpel tunnel surgery, but I thought rushing into something like that without more investigation seemed wrong. For advice, I called my brother Paul, a researcher in neural anatomy at Mt. Sinai Hospital in New York. He told me that I had injured an "uninteresting nerve," so no one knew much about it.

"The best neurologist in Belgium is visiting my boss, right now," Paul said. "You should go see him when he gets back to Europe next week—his office is in Antwerp,"

The neurologist's office was in an old Victorian house in the middle of the city about an hour north of us. The equipment and examining room were Spartan, like something out of the nineteenth century, different from the friendly doctors' offices I was used to. It was an adventure being there—although not one I wanted to have when I was feeling vulnerable from pain. But the neurologist was friendly and spoke English, explaining everything he was doing as he examined me. He said he didn't know why I was having so much pain.

"This is not a carpel toon-nul," he said and sent me over to the hospital for further tests.

Before I left, the neurologist handed me a bill and I handed him $20 worth of Belgian Francs. It was novel to hand a doctor cash—and such a small amount, too, for so thorough an exam. So many things in Belgium were expensive but health care was a bargain.

The hospital tests were another adventure, again in Antwerp in Spartan rooms with frightening looking equipment. Everyone was kind and spoke English to me but, when they talked to each other, they spoke Flemish—a language that I thought sounded like German. There I was, people sticking probes into my hand, attaching electrodes and putting electricity through my body, speaking a guttural language I couldn't understand. Alarmed, I felt like I had wandered into a German war movie. I was wild-eyed and jumpy when Josh came to get me after the tests.

"What's the matter?" He was worried.

"No-oo-oo-thing," I quavered, looking frantically all around and behind me, every muscle jumping wildly.

The tests were inconclusive, borderline carpal tunnel, and no one suggested surgery. They sent me home with a spray analgesic that I could get refilled at the local drug store without prescription. As I left, after hours spent in the hospital, I gave the cashier $35 in Belgian Francs, paying for all the tests.

* * *

At Christmas we went home to Connecticut for two weeks, our whole family glad to be back in our own beds. We relaxed at a bone-deep level; all of us recognized the layer of tension present in our lives in Brussels. The kids got to visit their old school, spending the few days with their friends. Then my Jewish sister-in-law hosted Christmas dinner, to my undying gratitude, picking up the ball when life was too frenzied for me to carry it. She had never hosted the holiday before; it was a true act of charity.

Christmas was bright for us that year, home after eight months away, but it wasn't so happy at Multiflow. DEC suddenly pulled back from the contract negotiations that Josh and the company had been involved in for more than a year. This was unexpected and, since cash was getting shorter, the future started looking grim. In a panic, some of the VCs suggested taking the company public right away, despite its lack of profits. In this crisis, it looked as though Multiflow needed Josh in the States more than it did in Europe and, before we left Connecticut, we picked up forms to enroll the kids in school, should we soon be brought home permanently.

Then the next month, after we were back in Brussels: "We're going home in February," Josh told me.

And I was taken aback; I didn't expect it to be this soon.

"Let's wait and tell the kids after Dorothy's birthday," I said. "Her party needs to be happy—not filled with sadness about her leaving." It was only a couple of weeks away.

Dave was thrilled when he found we were going home. But Dorothy became pensive and went to the piano, playing for a long time. She wanted to go home, but her friends at the ISB were important to her. She knew her chances of seeing them again were very small.

* * *

When people at home asked me if I liked living in Europe, I never knew what to say. There was no "yes or "no" answer. I liked so much about European life: the food, the travel, the discoveries in my French class and on the streets. But I never felt completely comfortable. I saw a rich life that I could never quite reach—it was very frustrating.

Since leaving Europe I have had a chance to think about my experiences there and ask myself what we learned and what we accomplished. We had had big ideas when we arrived: Josh wanted to open up Multiflow's European operations and collect the debt from the Wallonian region, and he reached those goals. But what I wanted to do was harder, more intangible. I thought I could master another culture, learn the language and bring my children into another world. But we were there such a short time, too short really, for such ambitious plans; we left not even having stayed a year.

One of the most surprising things I learned while we lived in Brussels was how American I am, in ways I never expected. At home, I only saw the differences between me and the people around me. In Europe, though, not only did people look at me and see an American, I saw myself that way. Faced with a foreign culture, I saw how American my worldview was—in ways as small as body language or as big as national pride.

We brought a small American television from the US for the kids' video games, and when we found that it got Armed Forces TV, I was thrilled. *The Today Show, Oprah, Phil Donahue*: it was wonderful. I felt like I had been re-admitted to the national conversation, in touch with my culture in a way I had been deeply missing. I had no idea how important this was to me: certainly no idea that television would make a difference in my life. Yet there I was, glad for the Americanisms, irritated at the BBC that Dave watched on our Belgian TV, afraid that the kids would pick up British speech patterns and start saying, "The school have decided..."

And what about the kids? Was living in Brussels a good idea for them—did they learn anything they wouldn't have learned in the States? Well, yes and no. The ISB was their community and that was American, yet they did get outside. Dave had been impressed by the depth of the London Underground and its history, writing a school paper on its use as a bomb shelter during World War II—so some things took. And he enjoyed his school trip to Florence, really learning about the Renaissance in a way that he couldn't have in the States. Dorothy was too young to understand a lot of the history but she definitely got a taste for travel. And she made good friends from vastly different places, learning about other cultures from them.

* * *

Before we went back to the States, we drove down to Paris at the beginning of February for one last weekend. Josh and I liked exploring odd parts of Paris; we'd be sorry when it was no longer only a three-hour drive away. This time we were going to La Villette, the science museum that had just opened east of Montmartre.

The weather was blustery when we arrived in Paris, but it often was in the winter, so we didn't pay attention as we went into the museum. After a few hours, we had lunch, and when Dave finished, he headed back across the museum floor, around the open area beneath the atrium roof. We told him to stay just across from us, that we would catch up with him when we were finished eating.

A few minutes later we noticed a commotion near the atrium and a lot of shouting. We ran out into the open area—what could be happening? Dave was on the other side of whatever it was and the guards were trying to get us to leave the museum, evacuating everyone. The glass atrium roof had broken—entire panels were falling out of their frames, shattering on the ground. But we didn't have Dave. Where was he? We needed to get to him—fast.

La Villette is a French science museum—not a word of English anywhere; we had spent the entire morning speaking French. Now, in trouble, we started yelling, telling everyone about our twelve-year-old son caught on the other side of the rubble. And our French was failing us.

Suddenly, with a child in danger, everyone spoke English. It was the most amazing thing. They came out of the woodwork to help—the place was transformed. People on all sides had things for us to do, suggestions to help us; I was overwhelmed by their kindness.

Guards took Josh to find Dave, and Dorothy and I were herded with everyone else out onto a balcony and then down emergency stairs. We went past the coat check area where everyone grabbed their coats which were laid out on the counter; then we went outside.

Once outside, it was easy to understand what was happening. The winds, which had been blustery before, were now literally hurricane force. La Villette was newly opened, with some parts still under construction. Debris was everywhere. Bits of masonry from the ancient buildings nearby had blown into the atrium roof, breaking the glass. It was all a mess.

La Villette is big, twice as big as the Smithsonian Air and Space Museum; there was no way for Dorothy and me to find the rest of our family once we were separated, without cell phones. And Dorothy was hysterical.

"I don't want to be a widow child," she screamed, disconsolate.

But there they were, waiting for us by the La Villette Metro station. Dorothy went running to Dave. He and Josh were happy to see us—and to have their coats back in the February cold.

Exhausted and relieved, we headed downstairs to the Metro. We went to a bar in the station where the kids had ice cream. The adults needed a drink.

We later learned that thirty people were killed in France during this freak storm with winds reaching 100 miles an hour. They were hit by concrete falling from seventeenth century buildings, and in southern England, four more people were killed and wind overturned trucks. The newspapers called it a super-tempest—winds strong enough for debris to break a tempered glass roof.

France bent under super-tempest;
overturned truck in England

THE END

We moved home from Brussels at the end of February, 1990, with raising money the most important thing Josh had to do. There had been a big setback with the DEC negotiations at Christmas, but since problems like that weren't unusual, I didn't give it very much thought. The company had always gone from financing to financing, looking for more investment dollars to hold them until sales could make them profitable. After the heady early years when the sky was the limit, Multiflow often felt shaky. I knew this wasn't sustainable, but I thought this reversal was more of the same—not a major threat.

During the months we were in Brussels, Multiflow management's energy had been focused almost entirely in one direction—the DEC deal. Negotiations started in mid-1988 when some of the Multiflow guys got together with their friends at DEC—the architects who had worked on the original DEC VAX, market leader in the minicomputer industry—to discuss ways the two companies could work together. It was a small community.

DEC wanted a product for the higher powered computer market, more powerful than the current VAX. DEC tried to develop a product internally, the VAX 9000, but it wasn't going well. The new design had powerful hardware but with little architectural innovation over the original VAX— and the original people were not involved. DEC management knew even as the team worked on it that it would be outdated before they could introduce it.

In the face of the problems with the 9000, the DEC engineers proposed that they and Multiflow start a serious level of collaboration to develop a jointly designed VLIW mini-supercomputer as a DEC product. The resulting machine would be a candidate for DEC's next important product, its entry into the high powered computer market. In addition, some people, particularly John O'Donnell, talked about putting VLIW technology on a chip as a way to combat the killer micros. He thought that large computers might be dinosaurs, but with money short at Multiflow, a joint project with DEC was the only way to do long term development. There was a lot to work out, requiring serious manpower from both companies. It was a project with many parts—one that could change both organizations.

Leigh coordinated for Multiflow and Bruce Collier for DEC, making sure the technical guys met all the milestones while contract negotiations went forward. There were a lot of terms to work out: How would the marketplace be divided after the product was introduced? What should DEC pay for Multiflow's expertise? And what about the intellectual property? It was very complicated.

The deal had a high profile within DEC because the architecture stars, the beloved designers of the early VAXes—Joel Emer, Tryg Fossum and several others—championed it. Sam Fuller, Vice President of Research, and Joe Zeh, head of architecture, also pushed for the deal. Several internal software stars—bright, forward thinking engineers—also backed it, but these guys left DEC, the leader, Dave Cutler, going to Microsoft to lead the project that developed Windows NT.

The chief opposition to the collaboration came from those working on the 9000, Bob Glorioso's team, powerful people within DEC. They thought that their product's hardware could shine in the marketplace—that it wouldn't be as bad as it appeared. But since the DEC technical stars wanted to talk to Multiflow, they went along with the negotiations.

DEC spent a lot of time evaluating Multiflow's technology to make sure it performed the way it was supposed to—as was appropriate for such a significant investment, one that might become an important product. This was mostly engineers sitting at desks with Rich Lethin, the hero of the Trace 300 series, as liaison doing a lot of the work. He had left Multiflow to get his PhD at MIT and was living in Boston, convenient to DEC headquarters in Marlborough, MA. For several months he spent a few days a week working up there on Multiflow's behalf.

To test the VLIW technology, the DEC engineers mixed it in with some other projects. They paid Multiflow about $1 million over the course of a year for this and also to compensate for Rich's time—and Bob Nix's, Woody's and Geoff's; they also worked with the DEC engineers.

Josh was in the middle of negotiations as the two companies worked to hammer out terms, even when we lived in Europe. Periodically, there would be a rumor that Bob Glorioso was unsold, and Josh or Don would rush to a meeting. His team, the VAX 9000 crew, was represented on the project task force but since his opposition was so strong, the Multiflow people met with him separately from time to time, keeping him directly up to date. Often, Don or Josh were kept waiting for hours, even though they had scheduled appointments; the politicization seemed petty but they tried to meet with Glorioso as much as they could to blunt the opposition. Josh would time his trips to the

States from Brussels around these meetings; this was where he was headed when he almost missed his flight in Amsterdam, detained as a suspicious person with a ticket bought that same day, traveling with only a briefcase.

The technical evaluation succeeded gloriously, the VLIW technology performing fully as well as Multiflow claimed. And because of this, the negotiations went well and the agreement took shape. Multiflow would get $10 million when DEC signed the contract, with more to come when the new product paid off. The two companies would divide the market for mini-supercomputers, with DEC aiming at the higher performance end, leaving Multiflow to market to the lower end. This would be a real change for Multiflow, a different business plan, with the company very much in DEC's orbit. They were willing to make this change because they were running out of alternate ways to finance the company; with the DEC deal, they would survive and have a steady stream of income.

Then, in October, 1989, the DEC VAX 9000 limped into the marketplace, as weak a product as everyone expected. Right away it looked like a failure—a computer very few people wanted, but Glorioso's team pushed to give it a chance. It didn't help that the economy was still bad, left over from the crash of 1987, and few companies were buying computers. Also, the killer micros were on DEC's tail, further reducing customers for a product costing the VAX 9000's $1.5 million.

And compounding the VAX 9000 debacle, DEC was having money problems, missing their financial projections which depressed their stock price. To Multiflow it looked as though DEC, faced with this embarrassing failure, needed a Trace product even more. But DEC didn't see it that way.

As the DEC/Multiflow deal neared the point of signing, the 9000 people within DEC redoubled their efforts against it. They had never liked the idea, wanting the 9000 to be the sole high-performance product, and as signing approached, they pushed back harder. To support them, they had two consultants, Yale Patt and Dave Patterson, leading lights in superscalar architecture, the dominant form in modern computers. They believed that VLIW was not the answer, despite how strong the technical evaluation results had been. Glorioso's team pushed and the consultants pushed, anxious that DEC not team up with Multiflow.

Just before Christmas, 1989, DEC sent word that they would not sign the deal that quarter. With the 9000 failure tugging at their financials, they would have had to report a quarterly loss if they now had to write off Multiflow's $10 million as an R & D expense. They had never had a losing quarter, and they couldn't face the thought of one now. They did not promise, but said that the next quarter might be different; they might sign the deal then.

DEC's not signing was a real blow. Multiflow had expected to close the deal that month, counted on the infusion of money. This was the deal they had staked their future on, neglecting everything else. It was brinkmanship, and money was tight. Multiflow could see it running out.

When we moved back from Brussels, Josh jumped right in, working to salvage the DEC deal. He pushed for a resolution, saying that a small company like Multiflow couldn't be left hanging. He was constantly in Marlborough or on the phone, trying to get the deal to come together. And he worked to find money elsewhere too, trying to pull something out of thin air, mining all his contacts. He and Leigh even started writing the IPO; though, at this point, it was too late for a public offering to serve their immediate cash needs since it took so long and cost so much money. It had always been a "Hail Mary pass," since they were not profitable, but the VCs said it might work, so he and Leigh worked on it.

Then, on March 26, 1990, DEC notified Don that they were withdrawing from all negotiations with Multiflow. And just like that, the deal was dead.

Felda Hardymon and Jim Morgan, two of the original Multiflow VCs, immediately raced to Marlborough for five hours of meetings to see if they could save it. But the deal was really dead. No amount of reviving worked.

Faced with the collapse of negotiations, no cash resources and no prospects for near-term cash, the Board voted to shut the company down. Multiflow was out of business.

* * *

After the Board decision, Josh called to tell me the news. He said they couldn't salvage the DEC deal, and now it was over—Multiflow was gone. After all we had poured into the company over the last few years, now there was nothing.

Shock ran through me as we talked; I had trouble taking it in. I knew things were shaky, but I wasn't prepared to hear what Josh was telling me. I was disoriented, having my world torn apart, too numb then to feel the pain and sadness that would come later. I put down the phone and just stood there.

After we hung up, Josh sat at his desk staring into space until the office wound down for the day. Then he went into the company kitchen where he found Ruttenberg, O'Donnell and Nix. They were the founders and the first employee to join the start-up and now their dreams for Multiflow were gone. Josh stayed in the kitchen with them into the evening, eating large bowls of popcorn, all of them making macabre jokes, conducting a funeral for their dreams with gallows humor. Before he left the office, Josh started his usual clean-up of the mess they left in the kitchen, but after a few minutes he stopped. He was drained and it all seemed pointless. He had a lot bigger messes to clean up. He left the kitchen and, in a spirit of absurdity, sent a juvenile memo to the people who ran the facility, complaining about the mess "some kind of pigs" had left behind.

When Josh got home that evening, we spent a lot of time crying. Our world had gone into freefall—we were shocked, horrified, despairing, feeling lost and very, very sad—so many emotions whirling around together. We called our families and told the kids. Everyone cried with us, the kids more disoriented than anything.

Josh never expected that DEC would turn Multiflow down flat. And I never realized how quickly it could all end. I kept expecting that something would happen to make it right, or that it had all been a mistake. Multiflow had been our lives for so many years, and now it was gone. So much was flashing through my mind and body that I had difficulty catching my breath. It wasn't the loss of possible wealth that threw me; those dreams had faded gradually as Multiflow ran into trouble. It was the loss of so much of my world. I kept shaking my head, trying to bring myself back into the present, to realize that it was actually happening.

The next day at Multiflow, March 27, 1990, Don and Josh held a company meeting. People stood or sat on the floor, some perched on equipment in the manufacturing area, the only place big enough to hold the entire company. Josh told everyone that the DEC deal was dead and there were no other places they could turn. Multiflow had run out of money; they were out of business. He said that they were all fired—himself included—and talked about how sad this made him, telling them again what amazing things they had all accomplished at Multiflow.

Reaction was subdued. Many people knew that the company was thrashing, especially since the DEC setback at Christmas, but no one had expected such a sudden jolt. Some people cried, and Josh was teary himself. People wandered around, calling their families or standing in clusters. Business was officially suspended.

As news trickled out, Josh began to get sympathy calls from colleagues and people he had worked with throughout the industry. Everyone knew about the promise of the technology and how good the Trace was; they were shocked. As a private company, Multiflow had no reporting obligations so no one knew how precarious the finances were.

That evening Ron Greuner, the Chief Technical Officer of Multiflow's competitor Alliant, called Josh at home from an airplane.

"I'm supposed to say 'sorry,'" he said, "but, I have to tell you; I'm actually sorry. I thought you guys were terrific people with great technology—I'm sad to see you go. I don't know if it's what you want but if it is, there's a place for you at our company, doing what you did at Multiflow."

Josh was touched and flattered, and he thought about Ron's call. He saw the start-up life starkly: Ron Greuner was calling from an airplane because his time was so valuable he couldn't waste a minute of it. He realized that Multiflow had been an amazing ride, but some part of him was relieved that it was over, that he was liberated from the grueling roller-coaster world of a start-up.

After he hung up, he turned to me. "Maybe I'll never have to make another telephone call from an airplane," he said.

The next morning we woke up to find Multiflow on the front page of the *New Haven Register*. Panicked, we ran to the kids' school. Dave was already upset, and his sixth-grade class reviewed current events every day, using the newspaper. We were afraid the teacher would unknowingly talk about the company, causing Dave even more pain. But the teacher was sympathetic, avoided the subject in class, and the issue passed uneventfully.

From the school, I went home but Josh went in to work—at Multiflow, the way he always did. When he got there, he was surprised to find that many other people had come in, too, almost all of the engineers, to finish up their work or do other things. Everything seemed normal, as though nothing had changed. It was eerie—like the Phony War before World War II actually broke out—but also emotional, no one knowing quite what to say to each other.

After that, the building stayed open for weeks to anyone who had a key—most of the employees. And many still kept coming in. Some had work to do helping dissolve the company, and some were hired by Prudential, the investor with ownership rights to the next Multiflow product; they wanted to whip it into shape so that they could try to sell it. But some people came in because this was where they worked and they needed to be there—it was rough letting go of a dream. And Multiflow had been a dream for a lot of people.

After a while, though, the reality of Multiflow's ending sank in and everyone started talking about other jobs. A group of about 40 engineers, including the founders and Leigh, decided they wanted to continue working together and courted companies to take them all. John Ruttenberg hired a team-building consultant to help them figure out how this could work and for about three weeks they tried to make it happen.

Alliant, Intel, Hewlett-Packard, Cray and DEC all sent recruiters to meet with the team but none of the companies could commit to taking that many people. Thinking Machines tried the hardest, talking for weeks about hiring the group, but when even they decided they couldn't take everyone, the idea of staying together died.

Bob Colwell needed a job with good health insurance because Ellen was pregnant—they couldn't afford to wait any longer. And neither could anyone else and, as time passed, the need became more urgent. The group began to disperse.

Josh, too, began looking for a job in earnest and we faced life as it was. To my bemusement, my mother-in-law sent us grocery coupons to help with finances.

And Dorothy consulted her friends about jobs. Their fathers were mostly doctors and dentists, and Dorothy had always hated that she couldn't describe what her father did for a living. She was worried, and had an idea for a fresh start.

"My friends think this is Dad's chance," she said. "Maybe he can get a real job, now—you know, like a pizza baker." She really thought she was onto something there.

* * *

As Josh was looking for a job, he was also working with the VCs selling off Multiflow assets and licensing the technology, reaping as much value from the company as they could. Josh wanted an orderly shut-down; it was in his best interest, since he wanted the technology spread as broadly as possible. But also, he cared about Multiflow as a company, had for six years and, despite his relief at the end of the rat race, he wanted the end to be as graceful as possible.

But dismantling the company was complicated. Multiflow used its last financial reserves to pay employee salary and expenses, but no one had thought about the vacation days the employees had earned. And this was a lot of money since Multiflow had been so intense that few people took vacations—Josh included. He was horrified to find that Connecticut state law considers this debt something outside the corporate shield, money that the company officers owed personally, a felony if it wasn't paid. A frightening story in the *New Haven Register* made this public and we worried obsessively.

Then one of the VCs suggested that Josh might be personally liable for all of Multiflow's debts, scaring him, although he was pretty sure it couldn't happen.

"I never signed personal guarantees; they can't come after my house." he said. "What are they thinking?"

I was thrown and momentarily terrified. What a horrible threat. But then I thought about it and realized it was just a VC tactic. They had no idea how much Multiflow meant to Josh, no idea that he would work for the company whether or not he was being paid. They thought they had to threaten him with bankruptcy to get his help.

"If the Masters of the Universe want to get you, they will," I said, "but I don't think we need to worry about this.

"Now that you're not going to get rich from Multiflow, they think you'll just run off. They're trying fear now, to get you to stay—since they don't have any more money to dangle. But getting rich was never your biggest goal. You always took care of Multiflow. Just keep doing it the way you always have and we'll probably be okay."

Luckily, money started tricking in at a crucial time and these concerns disappeared. Hewlett-Packard, Intel and DEC all bought technology licenses and paid promptly. And the VCs sold the Multiflow service business and the inventory of Traces to Bell Atlantic. Steve Eskenazi, the Service Manager, and most of the service people went with the inventory, too, so the service people got to stay together, even if the engineers didn't.

But a lot of the money they needed to avert danger came from European Trace sales that closed after Multiflow went out of business—even though the buyers knew that the company was gone. Chris Chaney and the European sales force Josh worked so hard to establish came through just when it was needed the most. Multiflow paid all the money owed to the employees for back vacation. And it paid enough of Multiflow's other debts that the creditors never forced it into bankruptcy.

In a follow-up article on Multiflow's shutdown, the *New Haven Register* said that the Attorney General of Connecticut "did not intend to indict the Multiflow officers" over the vacation pay. We were glad to hear this, but we didn't like the implication. That article left such a scar that now I look at articles that report such things and wonder about the stories behind them. The people involved sound like bad actors and I knew how far Multiflow stretched to make sure everything was done fairly, especially for the employees.

* * *

Did the VCs shut Multiflow down too quickly, without looking enough places for further financing? Or did Don's ego stop them from finding a buyer before it was too late? Would it have made a difference if Don had stopped being CEO after the product introduction or if they had started with Josh's lower computer price structure? Josh thinks so—that lower prices might have had given them a chance for success. That greater sales might have provided the profitability needed to hold on and make a chip using

VLIW technology when the time was right. Maybe—but it is hard to tell what might have happened.

Or maybe DEC killed Multiflow? For many years I thought they were to blame and adamantly opposed Josh's ever working there. Now, though, I think it was a lot more complicated than that. Multiflow had bad luck, a bad economy and the failure of a final deal that was just the last of many deals, none of which had been enough. For them to be successful, it would have taken hundreds of millions of dollars and even then it might not have worked.

In the 1980s there was incredible change in the industry—far bigger than anyone saw coming. Microprocessors so popularized computers that very soon everything had to be compatible. Programs that ran on one type of computer had to run on them all, and Multiflow could not adjust. The company was founded just after the time when it was possible for a new company to produce incompatible computers and succeed. Some large existing companies were still designing and successfully selling them to their customer base; if the DEC deal had happened and the Trace had become a DEC product, it might have succeeded, too.

But none of the new companies, the ones started after 1980, survived and on its own Multiflow couldn't have, either. One by one, the mini-supercomputer companies all died: Alliant and all the rest. Convex was last mini-supercomputer company to fail. It was acquired by HP, which had already bought Apollo. Later, Compaq bought DEC, then HP bought Compaq. And now HP makes mostly PCs and peripherals, all compatible products based on microprocessors.

* * *

At Christmas, 1990, nine months after Multiflow went out of business, the three founders, led by John Ruttenberg, sent a memento to all the Multiflow employees, investors, and friends. It was a small tombstone made of clear Plexiglas encasing a fragment of code.

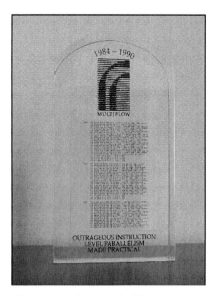

**The inscription reads, "Outrageous
Instruction Level Parallelism Made Practical"**

The letter the founders sent with the tombstone included these words:

"...For many of us, the time we spent together epitomizes how rewarding and fun work can be. Perhaps our greatest sadness is that our wonderful team is scattered, placing many of our best friends so far away. Bellwether projects such as Multiflow are rare, and all three of us feel lucky to have been associated with one in our lifetimes."

EPILOGUE

The Multifloids spread throughout the computer industry, making it better wherever they went, many of them preaching the VLIW religion. John Ruttenberg joined Silicon Graphics, carrying the compiler tradition as he went and so did Paul Rodman, Doug Gilmore and Woody Lichenstein. For many years, Paul Rodman's California license plate read "1ST VLIW."

Geoff Lowney and Bob Nix went to DEC to work on a new architecture using the Multiflow compiler. Bob Colwell and Dave Papworth went to Intel, joined there after a few years by Paul Rodman. Bob, Dave and Geoff all became Intel Fellows, though Geoff was a Compaq Fellow first, having changed companies twice without changing offices when Compaq acquired DEC and then Intel acquired his part of Compaq. In 2005 Bob Colwell, who by then had been Chief Architect for four of Intel's Pentium processors, won the Eckert-Mauchly Award—the highest award in computer architecture, previously won by scientists such as Maurice Wilkes, Gordon Bell, Seymour Cray and Gene Amdahl.

When Leigh and several of the more junior engineers joined start-ups right after Multiflow went under, I worried because I knew it was such a grueling life. But Josh reminded me how much younger than us these guys all were, that they were only taking the same chance we took years earlier when we were their age. Sure enough, Leigh went on to lead corporate development at research labs at Hewlett-Packard and IBM. Today he directs technology commercialization at the University of Wisconsin/Madison and is an officer of the university.

Brian Cohen, Multiflow's public relations guru who directed the Trace product introduction continued working with technology companies. Today he is Chairman of New York Angels Investor Marketing Council and has had long-term arrangements with Sony and IBM. He developed the IBM Big Blue/Gary Kasparov Chess Match, voted best public relations program of 1998. And Trace Cohen, like his father, today does strategic PR for technology companies.

Brussels was only the first stop for Chris Chaney, who managed Multiflow Europe. He went back to England but then took a job with a Nigerian computer distributor, eventually becoming its president. Whenever we met over the years, he has had fascinating stories to tell us.

John O'Donnell started Equator Technologies when Multiflow went under, joined there by Ben Cutler and Cindy Collins, software engineers. Together they continued development of the Multiflow compiler, selling and supporting it, teaching companies like NEC and Fujitsu to use and modify it. A few years later, John's interests changed and he started building VLIW chips. He passed the Multiflow part of Equator to Rich Lethin who started Reservoir Labs. Today the Multiflow compiler is a small part of Reservoir's business but Rich maintains the legacy. He works not only with Cindy but with Stefan Freudenberger and John Ruttenberg, too.

Josh and I kept in touch with many Multifloids but after a few years, we lost track of John O'Donnell. Then, in October, 2007, Rich Lethin sent Josh an article about him from *Business Week*. He was involved in another start-up—his interests had turned to solar energy.

"It's perfect," said Josh, when he read it. "That's what John was put on this earth to do—save the world through technology."

The article described O'Donnell: "His enthusiasm is 'borderline wacko,'" it said, quoting an admirer. And we thought that John hadn't changed a bit.

O'DONNELL His enthusiasm is "borderline wacko," says an admirer

68 | BusinessWeek | October 15, 2007

John O'Donnell in 2007: says an admirer: "borderline wacko"

Bell Atlantic continued to provide sales and service for Multiflow systems long after the company's end. Steve Eskenazi reported in 1992 that they supported 75 systems worldwide, even continuing to sell left-over Traces—five new machines in 1991 and another five in 1992. These machines were used for years by corporations and universities, producing the same high performance they did when Multiflow sold them. According to John

O'Donnell, the Trace became the prime computing platform for John Pople's computational chemistry investigations, which won the 1998 Nobel Prize for Chemistry.

And today Intel still uses the Multiflow compiler; it has influenced its development efforts for decades. The compiler is still written in the original way that Ruttenberg devised; an early Equator licensee tried to rewrite it, to translate it into a modern computer language, but failed miserably. The language is so elegant and precise that it lives still—25 years later.

Hewlett-Packard used its Trace for many years. They bought it along with a technology license, and after its useful life was over, HP donated it to the Computer Museum in Mountain View, CA. It is there today, along with relics from many of the other mini-supercomputer companies, machines with no other place in today's world.

* * *

After Multiflow folded, there were rumors in the technical press that Josh was about to open a new company in Prime Computer's former office space on Route 495 outside of Boston, but he wanted no part of it. He didn't want to work at another start-up; the kind words from other entrepreneurs who wanted him to join their companies didn't sway him. He wanted to go back to the life of a researcher—work on his technology in a way he had been too busy for at Multiflow.

But Josh had been out of the academic world for six years—and that was a long time. Did anyone remember how good a researcher he had been? What did the computer science world think of him after so long? Would there be a job for him? Josh had been working so hard for years with his head down, so focused on Multiflow, that he no idea what kind of professional reputation he had.

We made a list of possibilities, all the universities with strong systems departments and industrial R&D labs too, places doing real research. And when he started looking, Josh found to his surprise that he was a star—there were jobs everywhere. Not at Harvard or MIT, since he wanted permanence, and they weren't offering tenure, nor at the Yale Computer Science Department, which had just been through a bruising tenure fight. But there were plenty of academic jobs available: Cornell, Northwestern, and Carnegie Mellon; he considered all these and more.

But thinking about the academic world, Josh remembered applying for grants, that raising money is central to the role of an academic. He had been doing so much of that at Multiflow. That wasn't what he wanted now; he wanted to get back to doing research himself. He interviewed at several industrial research labs and when he got to Hewlett-Packard, he stopped. HP wanted him to continue with his research and also open an East Coast lab in Boston in a few years, since they wanted to build VLIWs. And with HP Labs' other projects, there was a lot of breadth, a lot of areas for him to get involved in.

"That will keep you out of trouble," I told him. "We get to stay on the East Coast, and you won't have to raise money."

Our family moved to Brookline, MA, the same town on the Boston line where my brother and his family had lived when Josh invented trace scheduling. Josh spent one week each month in Palo Alto until he opened HP Labs Cambridge in 1993, and our whole family moved to California during those summers. After the frenzied travel of the last few years, this seemed easy by comparison.

I continued to do presentation graphics in Boston for years, having bought Mirage and my beloved Colormaster and digitizer from Multiflow. Several of Multiflow's investors were my clients and also Tufts University Medical School. I adapted my digitizer technique, stressing my shoulder instead of my wrist, exchanging carpel tunnel pain for rotator cuff pain, but I continued to work. Eventually, though, Microsoft's Power Point graphics package put me out of business, since this enabled my clients to easily do their own graphics. My shoulder and wrist pains subsided.

Our kids grew up happy and strong in Boston, Multiflow and our ten months in Brussels part of their history. Dave continued to be interested in computer science, having spent his childhood learning about it at the dinner table. His PhD thesis advisor was Olin Shivers who had been a student of Josh's in the Yale architecture and compiler classes. He was as rigorous with Dave as Josh had been with him.

Olin Shivers conferring Dave's PhD degree, May, 2010

In our new life in Boston, I missed Multiflow's glamour and excitement, but I liked the calm. I relaxed as I hadn't in six years. Josh was happier too, doing work he loved with less tension in his life. And I didn't miss the celebrity, liked the anonymity of going to restaurants where no one knew who I was and meeting people who did not instantly know who my husband was. I never wanted my family on a newspaper front page again.

* * *

As the Multifloids spread through the industry, so did the technology. Ownership of the compiler passed to a licensing company and, through them, to Intel, DEC, HP, Fijitsu, Hitachi, and Silicon Graphics, among others, as they bought licenses. And trace scheduling and VLIW technology ended up in processors throughout the industry, often not in the form the technology took at Multiflow. Descendants of VLIW spread beyond the original licensees to companies such as NXP, Analog Devices and Texas Instruments. Most VLIW applications eventually migrated to embedded processors, those integrated into a single chip. Incompatibility is less a problem on embedded chips because they do a narrow range of jobs—and are programmed only by the developer.

In 1993 Josh opened HP Cambridge Research Lab, joined there by Stefan Freudenberger and his beautiful DAG drawing. The lab, collaborating with ST Microelectronics, developed its own embedded VLIW processor, originally designed to provide the power needed by high-performance printers. The processor, Lx, resembles the Trace in its architecture, even more than other VLIW processors—on a chip only as big as your fingernail.

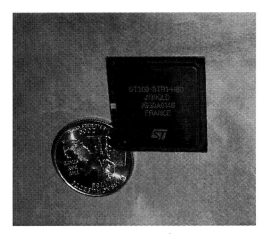

A prototype for Lx, the processor developed at HPLC, next to an American quarter. The actual processor is much smaller.

Many devices besides printers need the kind of computing power VLIW can provide, and today Lx is used in ST and HP products and licensed to companies worldwide. ST has shipped over 500 million Lx processors as of 2012 and still counting, with Lx into its second version now.

Multiflow sold only 140 computers but Lx, with over half a billion processors shipped, is used in all types of media processing, anything that needs a lot of power: printers, cable boxes, video devices, and DVRs. Besides the ST products, embedded VLIW processors from other companies, also shipped in the millions, are used in smartphones, computer graphics chips, cell base stations, GPS devices and hearing aids. Qualcomm's Snapdragon system includes multiple VLIWs. It is used in about half of the Android smartphones and tablets—and there are rumors of its inclusion in a future iPhone.

VLIW technology has come a long way from the days when scientists thought it wouldn't work. As Bob Colwell said, "If a VLIW family reunion were held today, every cell phone and media player would want to attend. Josh Fisher's vision and intellectual fearlessness in pursuing this unlikeliest of computer architectures are still paying off for the world today."

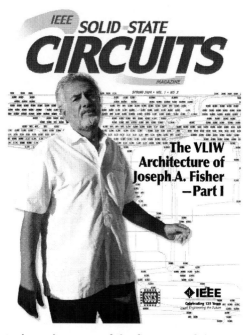

Josh on the cover of the first part of the IEEE
special issue about his technology, 2009

In 2003, Josh won the Eckert-Mauchly Award for his contributions to computer architecture, not only for the invention of VLIW but for his consolidation of the field of Instruction Level Parallelism. Then in 2005 he published a textbook, *Embedded Computing: A VLIW Approach to Architectures, Compilers and Tools*, co-authored with Paolo Faraboschi, the Lx Chief Architect, and Cliff Young. In 2009, three years after he retired as a Hewlett-Packard

Senior Fellow, the IEEE published a two part special issue on Josh's technology. Josh's article for the special issue was entitled *VLIW: From Blue Sky to Best Buy*. And In 2012 Josh won the IEEE Bob Rau award for computer architecture, an award named for his longtime colleague and competitor, now sadly gone.

And today Josh is fully retired, playing tennis every day in Miami Beach, FL and Asheville, NC. How does he do that in both places, exactly? Parallel processing—obviously.

TECHNICAL APPENDIX
WRITTEN BY JOSH FISHER

VLIW is a style of computer architecture that uses a form of parallelism called instruction-level parallelism to speed up the execution of programs. VLIW is an alternative to an older and more prevalent style called superscalar. To understand VLIW it is important to understand instruction-level parallelism in general as well as the contrast between VLIW and superscalar, and so this appendix explains all three concepts.

This description of VLIW technology has been written for the technically-oriented reader who would like to understand VLIW architectures better. It is not aimed at those with expertise in computer science. For those readers, there are Further Readings in the Sources chapter.

INSTRUCTION-LEVEL PARALLELISM

A program is a list of simple operations that the computer carries out in order to accomplish a task. Humans usually think of the computer as doing the operations one at a time, using what we call a machine cycle, or one tick of the computer's internal clock, for each operation. But most modern computers run programs in less time by overlapping operations, that is, starting one when earlier ones have not yet finished or even starting several at the same time. When a computer overlaps operations this way, and today almost all do, we say it is using *instruction-level parallelism (or ILP)*.

Suppose a computer is told to do the following simple operations in sequence:

(1)	C = A * B
(2)	F = D + C
(3)	W = X + Y
(4)	Z = P * Q
(5)	H = I + Z
(6)	K = L + Z

Figure 1. The original program.

In real computers, multiplications typically take longer than additions, so in this example we can think of (1) and (4) as taking two machine cycles and the additions as taking a single cycle. If no operations are overlapped, our example computer will use eight cycles to execute this program fragment (one cycle for each of the four adds, and two for each of the two multiplications).

But ILP can speed this up by overlapping the execution of operations. Can it overlap (1) and (2)? Certainly not, since (2) takes the number computed in (1)—that is, C— and uses it. We can see that (1) and (2) must be done *sequentially*, and in their original order, because (2) has to wait to start until (1) is finished, two cycles later.

But operation (3) has nothing to do with the first two, so it could be overlapped with either of them. Since modern computers use separate circuits to carry out addition and multiplication, most modern computers would be able to overlap the execution of (1) and (3). They can be carried out at the same time, or *in parallel*, in the first instruction.

Instruction 1	(3) W = X + Y		(1) C = A * B
Instruction 2			
Instruction 3	(2) F = D + C		

Figure 2: The first three operations would be executed in this time sequence.

Notice that we are referring to the simple program steps, (1)–(6), as *operations*, while we refer to a group of operations started at the same time as an *instruction*. In modern processors, ILP happens between many types of operations, not just adds and multiplies. It will overlap memory references, comparisons, and many others types of operations. And sometimes the designers of a computer will include multiple copies of the same hardware, in order to overlap several operations of the same type. In this example, we are defining the computer as having the hardware resources to initiate 2 additions or subtractions in the same instruction, but only a single multiplication.

Looking further down the original program, we see that (4) is unrelated to the previous operations, and could be done in Instruction 1. But (1) and (4) are both multiplications, and in this computer, there are only the hardware resources to start one multiplication in a given cycle, so one of those two operations will have to wait to be started. And (5) and (6) each use the result of (4), but are otherwise unrelated to any other operations; they could be started after the two-cycle (4) finishes. Thus we can use ILP to carry out the program in four cycles, getting a 2X speedup over the original eight cycles:

Instruction 1	(3) W = X + Y		(1) C = A * B
Instruction 2			(4) Z = P * Q
Instruction 3	(2) F = D + C		
Instruction 4	(5) H = I + Z	(6) K = L + Z	

Figure 3: All six operations would be executed in these four cycles.

One last detail about hardware resources: notice that our one multiplier starts (4) before it is finished with (1). The mechanism that allows it to start a new operation each cycle is called *pipelining*. It is similar to the pipelining found in auto factories, where each stage does the same thing to different cars as they go by. Most computers that use ILP offer pipelining for at least some long operations.

When programmers want to increase the ILP in their program, they often use an automated software tool that lets them visualize which operations have to wait for others, thus limiting ILP. The tool draws what is called a Directed Acyclic Graph (or *DAG*). A DAG is a picture that shows all of the operations in a program, with lines between any two where one must follow the other even when the program is rearranged. In Figure 4 there are edges between (4) and both (5) and (6) to show that (4) must be executed before both of them. DAGs for real programs, such as the DAG on Stefan Freudenberger's wall at Multiflow, often have thousands of nodes; here is the small DAG for the program fragment in Figure 1:

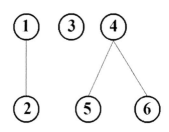

271

ILP is different from the usual thing called *parallel processing*. For example, modern dual-core and quad-core processors, as found in most modern laptops and even tablets and smartphones, carry out tasks in parallel. But these tasks are not simple operations like those above. They are large jobs given to separate complete processors that are able to operate independently from each other. ILP, instead, involves taking the small operations that are near each other in a single computation, and overlapping them.

A FUNDAMENTAL CHOICE: SUPERSCALAR VS. VLIW

Operations can only be overlapped if neither depends upon the other. But how does the computer know whether two operations can be overlapped? And how does it decide which to overlap? The process of determining which operations should be executed together, and in what order to execute them, is called *scheduling,* and the resulting execution order is called a *schedule*. Figure 3 is an example of a schedule.

Basically, there are two different approaches to when and how scheduling is done: the computer can figure it out on its own as the program runs, or the schedule can be figured out in advance, either by the programmer "by hand" or automatically by the compiler. When the compiler figures out the parallelism, it does so in addition to its usual job of translating the program from a high-level programming language into machine language.

In the first case, the program looks "normal" when handed to the computer. Like Figure 1, it is simply a list of operations to be executed. The computer examines the operations in the course of running the program. When it determines that operations can be overlapped and it decides it has the resources to overlap them, it makes the decision to overlap their execution on its own. To repeat:

the production of the schedule is done by the hardware as the program runs. Computers that make use of ILP this way are called *superscalar*.

In the second case, the program that the computer is given to execute already contains the information about what operations can be done together. This information has been added in advance by the software. The computer doesn't make decisions on its own; it simply does in parallel what the program tells it to do in parallel. The program is given to the computer in a form similar to Figure 3. The program is essentially the schedule, and the instructions are already "long," that is, they contain more than one operation in a single instruction. While a normal operation might be encoded into 32-bits, a long instruction, containing many operations, might be far longer—the Multiflow Trace had 1,024 bit instructions in its 28/300 model, and could encode up to 28 operations into a single instruction when it could find that much parallelism. Thus the name *very long instruction word or VLIW* is applied to computers that execute programs in this manner.

TRACE SCHEDULING AND THE PRACTICALITY OF VLIW

Superscalar-style ILP was first implemented about 50 years ago in the most powerful computers made then, including the CDC-6600 and the IBM 360/91. Computers with hardware that looked like VLIW, with the code hand-written (not produced automatically by a compiler) have been around almost as long, but the laborious code production process made them practical only for specialized use, involving small amounts of code that was run repeatedly.

VLIW vs. superscalar. The hardware in both is similar, and in both cases the compiler is given a program in a high-level language. In both cases, the compiler translates into machine-level code, but the VLIW compiler does the scheduling in advance

From the very beginning, ILP faced a fundamental limit in how much parallelism there was to exploit. That barrier was branches, that is, operations like (8) in this sequence:

(7)   C = A * B
(8)   if (C < D) branch to (2104)
(9)   W = X + Y

What is meant by (8) is that after doing (7), the computer should test whether C is less than D. If it is, then rather than carry out (9) next, the program continues at some other, far away point in the program, in this case an instruction found at (2104). But if, on the other hand, C is

274

not less than D, the program continues by executing (9) next.

Obviously, (7) and (9) can't be overlapped. If the branch, (8), is taken and the program continues elsewhere, (9) would not be executed. Overlapping them, without knowing whether the branch will be taken when the program runs, could lead to the wrong result. In general, this implies that there is no way to overlap operations that are found on opposite sides of a branch. But because branches typically occur every 5-8 operations and ILP that can be found in the code between branches—called a *basic block*—is severely limited, it would be great to find parallelism beyond basic blocks.

Trace scheduling, developed in 1978-9, is a compiler technique that addresses the branch problem before the program is handed to the computer. The compiler looks at a large section of code that includes many branches, and picks a path that it judges the program would be most likely to follow. That code is scheduled, branches and all, as if the compiler were sure that the code would go that way. Then extra operations are added to correct the computation when, at run time, the branches go in the unpredicted way. The process then repeats: a path is picked from the remaining unscheduled code, that path is scheduled, and so on, until all the code has been scheduled. Most branches go in one direction most of the time, and the compiler can usually predict which direction is more likely. As a result, the schedule that is produced contains a lot of useful ILP, much more than the hardware can find at run time.

Trace scheduling is useful for both VLIW and superscalar architectures, and has been used extensively for both. In VLIW architectures, the schedule becomes the actual program handed to the computer to execute. In

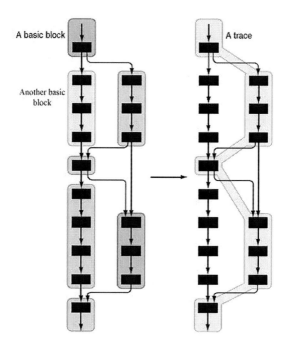

**An example of a path through the code that the
Trace Scheduler might take.**

superscalar architectures, the schedule is produced, but then it is turned back into a one-operation-at-a-time program, allowing the superscalar scheduling hardware to do what it does. Because of the rearrangement of the program made by trace scheduling, the superscalar hardware easily finds more ILP that it would have otherwise.

SUPERSCALAR AND VLIW TRADOFFS

Designers of new ILP-oriented computer architectures face the choice of VLIW vs. superscalar. The tradeoffs involved are subtle and many, with market forces and the momentum of existing architectures and engineering styles playing a major role.

Superscalars have the advantage that the same program can run on very different computers that execute the same repertoire of instructions. That is because the rearrangement isn't done in advance; in contrast, a VLIW's schedule must look just like the hardware, so it is necessary to recompile the program when even small details of the implementation change. This is the advantage of superscalars that has made them overwhelmingly attractive in the general-purpose processor space. Superscalars are also able to adjust their execution sequence to dynamic changes (for example, when a fetch takes a variable number of cycles) while the program runs, thus increasing performance. Finally, there is the fact that less compiling is required for a superscalar, since the hardware does part of the job. But because, in fact, the great majority of the work involved in compiling for these processors is a function of the ILP achieved, not of the processor's architectural style, this factor makes less difference than it seems. Superscalars simply offer less ILP than VLIWs, so require less compiling.

VLIWs have the advantage of requiring less hardware, lower power, and lower design cost and time. They are often easier to design and build than superscalars with similarly complex instructions, and are more easily mutable. That is, you can take a design of a VLIW processor and change it to a new, similar VLIW with less effort. All of these VLIW advantages arise from the absence of the superscalar's scheduling hardware, which can be complex, large, and power-hungry. Taken together, these advantages make it practical to build VLIWs that offer far more ILP than a superscalar can.

SOURCES AND FURTHER READING

Josh's and my memories were the most important sources for this book; we talked through the Multiflow years on all of our car trips for a year and a half—from Miami to Asheville, around Florida, or on our way to visit our daughter and son-in-law, Dora and Norman, in Chicago—recording our discussions as we drove. Most of the quotes I have used in this book were seared into our memories during the vivid Multiflow years.

The memory of other Multifloids was another important source; I spent hours on the phone with Rich Lethin and Geoff Lowney, and had email exchanges with Woody Lichtenstein and Bob and Ellen Colwell.

I have relied on published materials, too, particularly Rich Lethin's article in the IEEE Solid-State Circuits Magazine; *"How VLIW Almost Disappeared—and Then Proliferated,"* published in Summer, 2009, pp 15 - 23 and on an interview with Bob Colwell, published on-line as an oral history by ACM SIGMICRO, August, 2009. In addition, Josh's personal records include email from the Yale years, his calendar and log from our Brussels year. He also has access to Multiflow memorabilia—many memos and business plans—from all those years ago.

OTHER SOURCES:

Aviation Week & Space Technology, "Networking," pp 82-84, July 14, 1986

Bayot, Jennifer, "Derald H. Ruttenberg, 88, Quiet Deal Maker, Dies" New York Times; September 21, 2004

Brown, Chappell, "Supercomputers For Engineers On A Budget", Electronic Engineering Times, pp. 31, 47, January 26, 1987.

Business Week, "Developments to Watch," p. 79, March 10, 1986.

Ibid, "WILL MULTIFLOW SET A NEW STANDARD?," p.82A, April 20, 1987

Ibid; "THE HUNGRY PACK NIPPING AT CRAY'S HEELS," October 26, 1987.

Ibid, "Solar's Day in the Sun," p. 68, October 15, 2007.

BYTE, "Parallel Computer Uses 256-Bit Instructions," pp. 38 - 40, July, 1987.

CAE, "Near-Supercomputers Move into Engineering," pp. 89 - 94, July, 1987.

CIME, "Breaking the Barriers to Parallel Processing," pp. 10 -13, May, 1987.

Dickman, Steve, "GIVING COMPUTERS AN ELEPHANT'S MEMORY," Business Week, p. 50, September 1, 1986.

Digital Review, "Team Computing Garners Support: Multiflow Signs On," pp. 11-12, 14, January 15, 1990.

Electronic Business, "Nine for the next ten," p. 178, December 10, 1985.

Electronic Engineering Times, "SuperCPU Cranks Out 120 Mflops, Looks Ahead to Speed Execution,"; p. 1, 8, April 27, 1987.

Electronic News, "Multiflow Offers 64-Bit CPU Line," p. 12, April 27, 1987.

Greater New Haven Business Digest, "Multiflow hopes its super computers mean super growth," pp 3-5, January, 1988.

Hamilton, Rosemary, "Intel enlists Multiflow for parallel computer," Computerworld; February 12, 1990

Hemmingway, Brendan, "Yale designs supercomputer," Yale Daily News, pp. 1, 4. April 20, 1983

Ibid, "New plans for fast computing," Yale Daily News, p. 3, April 21, 1983.

Higgins, Carol B., "Computer whiz traces swift rise of Multiflow empire," INTERCORP, pp 14-27, April 15-26, 1988.

High Technology, "Multiflow Computer: ENTERING THE MINI-SUPERCOMPUTER MARKET," p.71 Dec, 1985.

Le Journal du Dimanche, "La France a plié sous la supertempete," p. 3, February 4, 1990.

McClune, Jenny, "Multiflow Debuts Its Minisupercomputers," Computer System News, p. 14, April 27, 1987.

Meng, Brita, "Parallel Processing Makes Compiler Advances," ESSO: THE Electronic System Design Magazine, pp. 61 - 65, March, 1987.

Montgomery, John I., "VERY LONG WORDS AT VERY FAST SPEEDS," Digital Review, p 27 - 31, January 15, 1990.

Parallelogram; Interview with Josh, pp. 14-16, January, 1990.

PC Informatique, "Métrologie prend le large," July 10, 1989.

Technotime; "1988 Hall of Fame for Engineering, Science and Technology HOFEST Inductees," p. 1, October, 1988.

Verity, John, "Follow the Herd," Venture, pp. 28-32, February, 1987.

Ibid, "A New Slant on Parallel Processing," Datamation; pp. 79-84 February 15, 1987.

FURTHER READING

A. E. Charlesworth, "An Approach to Scientific Array Processing: The Architectural Design of the AP-120B/FPS-164 Family," IEEE Computer, vol. 14, no. 9, pp. 18–27, Sept. 1981

Colwell et al. (1987). R. P. Colwell, R. P. Nix, J. J. O'Donnell, D. B. Papworth, and P. K. Rodman, "A VLIW Architecture for a Trace Scheduling Compiler," Proceedings of the 2nd International Conference on Architectural Support for Programming Languages and Operating Systems, pp. 180–192, Oct. 1987.

Colwell et al. (1988). R. P. Colwell, R. P. Nix, J. J. O'Donnell, D. B. Papworth, and P. K. Rodman, "A VLIW Architecture for a Trace Scheduling Compiler," IEEE Transactions on Computers, vol. 37, no. 8, pp. 967–979, Aug. 1988.

Colwell et al. (1990). R. P. Colwell, W. E. Hall, C. S. Joshi, D. B. Papworth, P. K. Rodman, and J. E. Tornes, "Architecture and Implementation of a VLIW Supercomputer," Proceedings of the 1990 International Conference on Supercomputing, pp. 910–919, Nov. 1990.

P. Faraboschi, G. Brown, J. A. Fisher, G. Desoli, and F. Homewood. "Lx: A Technology Platform for Customizable VLIW Embedded Processing," Proceedings of the 27th Annual International Symposium on Computer Architecture, pp. 203–213, June 2000.

J.A. Fisher, P. Faraboschi, and C. Young. "Embedded Computing: A VLIW Approach to Architecture, Compilers and Tools." Morgan Kaufman, 2004.

J. A. Fisher and B. R. Rau, "Instruction-level Parallel Processing," Science, vol. 253, pp. 1233–1241, Sept. 1991.

J. A. Fisher, "Very Long Instruction Word Architectures and the ELI-512," Proceedings of the 10th Annual International Symposium on Computer Architecture, pp. 140–150, June 1983.

J. L. Hennessy and D. A. Patterson. "Computer Architecture: A Quantitative Approach" 3d ed. Morgan Kaufmann Publishers (an imprint of Elsevier), 2003.

IEEE, "The VLIW Architecture of Joseph A. Fisher, Part 1", Solid-State Circuits Magazine, IEEE, 2009, Volume: 1 , Issue: 2

IEEE, "The VLIW Architecture of Joseph A. Fisher, Part 2", Solid-State Circuits Magazine, IEEE, 2009, Volume: 1 , Issue: 3

P. G. Lowney, S. M. Freudenberger, T. J. Karzes, W. D. Lichtenstein, R. P. Nix, J. S. O'Donnell, and J. C. Ruttenberg, "The Multiflow Trace Scheduling Compiler," Journal of Supercomputing, vol. 7, no. 1–2, pp. 51–142, May 1993.

B. R. Rau and C. D. Glaeser, "Some Scheduling Techniques and an Easily Schedulable Horizontal Architecture for High Performance Scientific Computing," Proceedings of the 14th Annual Workshop on Microprogramming, pp. 183–198, Oct. 1981.

B. R. Rau and J. A. Fisher, "Instruction-Level Parallel Processing: History, Overview, and Perspective," The Journal of Supercomputing, vol. 7, no. 1–2, pp. 9–50, May 1993.

PHOTOGRAPHS

Images on the cover and all pictures, except those listed below, courtesy J. Fisher.

VLIW: *Yale Daily News*
Don Eckdahl: *Greater New Haven Business Digest*
Product Introduction: *Digital News*; *INTERCORP, Business Week.*
Europe: *Le Journal du Dimanche*
Epilogue: *Business Week*; *IEEE.*

ACKNOWLEDGEMENTS

My first "thank-you" is to Marian DelVecchio. In November, 2010, she asked me to be part of her writing group, and I thought, "Well, this will be fun—I'll get to know Marian better." I started slow, but soon I was amazed to find thoughts pouring out of me onto paper and I realized how much I loved writing. Thanks also to the rest of my writing group: Judy, Rachel, Tamara, and Shirley. I have learned an incredible amount from the different perspectives you bring to my work.

A very important thank you to Diane Goodman, writing teacher extraordinaire, who led our group for two years. With her background in poetry, Diane taught me, not just narrative style, but word placement and the flow of writing. She was with me during the first year I plowed through this book, encouraging me, bringing me up short, everything I needed. Any remaining awkwardness is in spite of her best efforts, not because of them.

Thanks also to my family and friends who were universally encouraging and listened to me talk endlessly about the book. And thanks to my readers: Leigh Cagan, John Campbell, Lauren Wohl, and Cliff Young. Their help guided me through this process. It was Cliff who suggested that I needed a chapter on building the Trace, which turned into two chapters. When I realized that neither Josh nor I had enough material for these technical chapters, because Josh was traveling so much when the Trace was being built, I went to the Multifloids. Thank you to Rich Lethin and Geoff Lowney, both of whom spent hours with me on the phone. And to Leigh Cagan, Woody Lichtenstein and Bob and Ellen Colwell, all of whom provided help by email.

My last and most important thank you is to Josh who is, of course, the inspiration for this book. He has been with it every step of the way, as he has been with me in life. His patience explaining the technology cannot be overstated, since I am not a computer scientist and the technology is so subtle. This is not primarily a technical book, but because the technology is so important, I took great pains to get it right. My goal has been for Rich Lethin not to recoil in horror.

I apologize for inaccuracies in the technology; they are due to my naivety and happened in spite of Josh's best efforts. He would sometimes throw up his hands and let me continue with my oversimplifications because he knew how much I wanted to write this book. I am grateful for his patience, now and always.